Vietnam War

The Story of an Infantryman in Vietnam War

(A Blue-collar Kid's Journey to the Vietnam War and Back)

Sandra Koch

Published By **Simon Dough**

Sandra Koch

All Rights Reserved

Vietnam War: The Story of an Infantryman in Vietnam War (A Blue-collar Kid's Journey to the Vietnam War and Back)

ISBN 978-1-77485-761-8

No part of this guidebook shall be reproduced in any form without permission in writing from the publisher except in the case of brief quotations embodied in critical articles or reviews.

Legal & Disclaimer

The information contained in this ebook is not designed to replace or take the place of any form of medicine or professional medical advice. The information in this ebook has been provided for educational & entertainment purposes only.

The information contained in this book has been compiled from sources deemed reliable, and it is accurate to the best of the Author's knowledge; however, the Author cannot guarantee its accuracy and validity and cannot be held liable for any errors or omissions. Changes are periodically made to this book. You must consult your doctor or get professional medical advice before using any of the suggested remedies, techniques, or information in this book.

Upon using the information contained in this book, you agree to hold harmless the Author from and against any damages, costs, and expenses, including any legal fees potentially resulting from the application of any of the information provided by this guide. This disclaimer applies to any damages or injury caused by the use and application, whether directly or indirectly, of any advice or information presented, whether for breach of contract, tort, negligence, personal injury, criminal intent, or under any other cause of action.

You agree to accept all risks of using the information presented inside this book. You need to consult a professional medical practitioner in order to ensure you are both able and healthy enough to participate in this program.

Table Of Contents

Chapter 1: How It All Began 1

Chapter 2: Local Leaders Take Action....... 6

Chapter 3: Japanese Occupation............ 12

Chapter 4: France Tries The Steering Of The Tide 21

Chapter 5: Holding Back The Communist North 30

Chapter 6: The Vietnam War Summarized 142

Chapter 7: What Caused The War? 150

Chapter 8: Kennedy's Participation 158

Chapter 9: Johnson's Involvement 167

Chapter 10: The Downfall And War Crimes 179

Chapter 1: How it All began
Vietnam's Historical Conflict in Brief

Most people think of the Vietnam War in terms its history as a French colony. Then they forget about Vietnam's subsequent fall into the communist orbit. But Vietnam's struggle for independence is far more complicated than that. You must look at Vietnam's whole history to understand the reasons for the war.

Vietnam can be traced to its origins back to 2500 BCE. At that time, the nation was ruled by local potentates. These powerful men governed sprawling societies that largely revolved about rice patties. Vietnam was a peaceful nation until China, a juggernaut neighbour, made it impose its will on Vietnam.

In the North, the Nam Viet Kingdom was defeated. Vietnam would continue to be subordinated over 1000 years to China.

Vietnam fluctuated in that time between toeing the line, and times of explosive violence towards Chinese authority.

One of the most important of these revolts, which took place in 40CE was led and commanded by the Trung sisters. Vietnam's Trung sisters, Trung Trac Nhi (or Trung Nhi), are legends. Trung Trac, her older sister was the widow Thi Sach, who was a freedom fighter killed in battle. Her husband, who had plotted to overthrow Chinese rulership, was executed by China. Upon her husband's death, Trung Trac didn't just get bitter - she got even.

According to the official narrative Trung Trac and Trung Nhi led a massive rebellion in Vietnam against the Chinese. They marched on Chinese sites and forced their foreign counterparts to flee. The rebellion was short-lived. However, by 43 CE the Chinese had provided enough reinforcements for the end of the Trung uprising.

It is said that the Trung sisters chose to drown rather than surrender when they were attacked by enemy soldiers. Other stories say they were beheaded.

The Trung sister rebellion would most likely not be China's last, and China's dominion on Vietnam would be markedly affected by repeated attempts of Vietnamese freedom fighters.

Later rebellions against French and Japanese colonization efforts would mirror these homegrown insurgencies. Vietnam would eventually overthrow the Chinese yoke 939 CE. They would also resist repeated Chinese attempts to reaffirm the Chinese yoke during the subsequent years.

Vietnam would be divided into two states in the interim. South Vietnam was ruled in part by a military-elite that believed in a feudal system based on close family ties. North Vietnam, on the other hand, was a distinct regime that was heavily influenced by

Confucian ideas and was closer to China. The ideological split between North Vietnam and South Vietnam which would lead to the rise of communism in the region during the 20th century was largely due the existence of divisions hundreds of decades ago. Vietnam had two separate kingdoms prior to the French invasion.

Napoleon III, a nephew of Napoleon Bonaparte and the French ruler Napoleon III was the one who led the charge in Vietnam to seize the territory. Napoleon III, the president and vice-president of France, had previously served a term which was intended to last from 1848-1852. The French Constitution of the time prohibited an incumbent president from seeking a second term. Napoleon III, however irritated by his plans being cut short, organized a successful coup to install him as "emperor" of France in December 1851.

Napoleon III was inspired by Napoleon Bonaparte to seek expansion of France's colonial kingdom. In summer 1857, a push to expand France's colonial empire led to an invasion of Vietnam's agriculturally-rich southern region. They were "outgunned" by the French but the Vietnamese resistance was so strong that the French invaders had to wait until the summer in 1862 before they could defeat the southern Vietnamese forces.

The French launched an assault on Hanoi, the northern Vietnamese capital city, in 1882. French control also came to the north and central regions in Vietnam. France consolidated its control further over the next decade by adding Laos from Southeast Asia to its "Indochinese Union," a group it created in 1887.

Chapter 2: Local Leaders Take Action

The Vietnamese people began to resist French rule after decades. Many of these early freedom activists were from North Vietnam. They had been raised in France during the latter decades of the 19th-century. They began to organize their own resistance as early as the 20th century. Realizing that physical force was futile in the face of well-armed Frenchmen, they began to subtly call this resistance reform.

Vietnam took its inspiration from Japan's rapid modernization under the Meiji Restoration. It wanted to be Westernized in order to achieve their own restoration.

The Civilization of New Learning was an anonymously-written publication that emerged as one of the initial fruits of these efforts in 1904. The author made it clear why Vietnam had been slow to progress and shared their ideas on what was necessary to allow Vietnam to become modern. The writer stated that Vietnamese civilization had become stagnant, and needed an injection of rigor & ingenuity like the one Western civilization received. A simple formula for social progress was discovered by the writer that would help Vietnam overcome its current problems. Or, as an anonymous author said, "the greater the number of ideas, the higher the competition; the higher the level of competition, and vice versa."

It was a powerful, simple sentiment that mobilized many Vietnamese leaders to pull Vietnam from its feudal woes and help it become a more competitive nation full of new ideas. This intellectual movement, which was led by young reformers seeking to make a profound change in Vietnamese society, had been cultivated into a national phenomenon by the 1920s.

French tried to curb political activism. They often made arrests or even expelled people. Ironically, however, it was the French education system that kept producing the rabble rousers that the colonial governments were so opposed to. The Vietnamese intelligentsia, who had been educated in college, had limited options for employment. They could accept low-level jobs in the government or push for greater reforms to the colonial system. Many chose the latter.

French officials, however, struggled to decide between tightening regulations and increasing crackdowns. One of these loosenings on the colonial reins resulted in a publishing boom at the end of the decade with a wide range of pamphlets.

This literature often referred to the great philosophical works of thinkers like Friedrich Nietzsche. Baruch Spinoza. Immanuel Kant. It would be the former and the communist ideals of he espoused that would truly gain acceptance among the Vietnamese intelligentsia. Ho Chi Minh (the future communist leader) created the Vietnamese Revolutionary Youth League (1925), which was directly related to Vietnamese communist activities in the region.

Ho Chi Minh was an infant born in the early 1800s. He grew-up under French dominion. When he was young, he traveled overseas and was present at the Paris peace conference after World War I. Many reform-minded Vietnamese hoped, after the end of World War I that the new international order this war had created would convince the major players to back Vietnamese independence.

Minh wrote a petition to Woodrow Wilson, asking for Vietnamese self-determination. These appeals failed to be heard for most of their time. Ho Chi Minh joined communism as a result. Minh in Vietnam was the Youth League's director. He then wrote "The Road to Revolution", his own communist manifesto.

This tract was evidence Minh's total transformation from communist sympathizer, to all-out communist ideology. French officials began to focus their attention on Minh and his Youth League towards the end. They considered it a threat against their dominion of Vietnam. Their concern was justified by Minh's 1930 founding of the Vietnamese Communist Party.

Although the majority of party members were initially from the Youth League, Minh saw a significant increase in his base after the Great Depression that struck the 1930s. Many peasant farmer became disillusioned by the inability to sell their rice crops suddenly and started to embrace the Marxist views of the communists. Minh's Organization helped the peasant crop to form "soviets," communist enclaves modeled after Russian communes.

Minh's communist outreach had been limited to the peasant and upper classes of Vietnamese society before Minh. Ho Chi Minh's outreach and support to Marx's

Vietnamese working class proletariat would prove much more successful then previous reform/revolutionary initiatives had been. This would only happen despite French attempts at stemming the tide. Minh's planned takeover of Vietnam would be a challenge for external forces other than French and Vietnamese.

Chapter 3: Japanese Occupation

1940 would bring France terrible circumstances. Germany was still reeling from World War I's defeat and had been saber rattling with its European neighbors throughout the 1930s. The Nazi's blitzkrieg began to wreak havoc on Western Europe by the summer 1940. France officially surrendered its territory to Nazi aggression June 22, 1940. The French reached an agreement in which they ceded northern France, already swarming by Germans, to Nazis.

Southern France was converted into an Axis satellite by the French government of Vichy. It was nominally autonomous and based out Vichy's new French capital. However, Vichy France was now fighting for the Axis powers Germany, Italy and Japan. The Japanese were hoping to seize the fragile French colonial influence in Asia.

While they couldn't invade and seize territory from an Axis power, the Japanese were willing to look for any excuse to do so. Japan demanded from France, shortly after Germany had surrendered, that they permit North Vietnam to receive troops. It claimed these troops were necessary for rapid deployment against China.

Japan had been fighting China in war since the 1930s. Seeing North Vietnam as an excellent platform to attack southern China, they requested that the French agree to their demands. The French did not have the luxury of being able to argue and allowed the Japanese to send thousands of soldiers to the region. The truth is, any bully who has ever had to deal will quickly make another demand.

Japan demanded control of Haiphong, the strategic Vietnamese port, shortly after the French allowed these Japanese troop deployments. Japan sent 10,000 troops into the region just a few days after issuing this ultimatum. Japan became the absolute authority in Vietnam. But they also left a skeleton team of colonial administrator to ensure that the civil structure was maintained.

But these French colonials were now directly subservient for the Imperial Japan interests and their Vietnamese counterparts most definitely took notice. Even though they were unable to expel the Japanese, Vietnamese communist ideologues started to organize their own resistance. Ho Chi Minh established the communist organization known as the "Viet Minh," in May 1941 to combat the fascism promoted by the Japanese.

Ho Chi Minh was said to have wanted to decrease the Marxist focus of class struggle and instead placed more emphasis upon Vietnamese patriotic traditions, in order to unify all Vietnamese against the French & Japanese. This mobilization by the Viet Minh to resist Japanese aggression would tap into a long line of homegrown uprisings that have been against foreign invasion. Ho Chi

Minh became more aggressive in its guerilla warfare with the Japanese and began to reach out towards both China (and the United States) for help.

Minh first came to know the U.S. Office of Strategic Services via his work with the latter. Ho became an OSS agent during World War II. (He was referred to by as Agent 19). Ho provided intelligence to American OSS officers about Japanese deployments in Vietnam and surrounding areas. In the meantime, Ho Chi Minh had an impressive following and was the number-one freedom fighter at Vietnam's end of World War II.

According to some accounts, Vietnamese peasants from the Red River Delta joined in their thousands with the movement as early as 1944. One of many factors that energized the peasantry the most was that the Viet Minh appeared to be the only ones on the ground with their best interests at heart. In the winter of 1944/45, there was a severe drought in the country.

However, the Viet Minh used the requisitioned merchandise to help the Vietnamese in times of famine. They led daring raids into Japanese supply depots. After having proven themselves to be their best benefactors, it isn't surprising that so much of the peasant population would form a solid solidarity with Viet Minh.

World War II was drawing to a close at this point and the Axis were facing certain defeat. Italy had been eliminated and Germany was losing ground to all its enemies. Japan, aware of their imminent Allied invasion, decided to secure Vietnam for themselves and keep this base in Southeast Asia.

So, on March 9th 1945, Japan dissolved French authority and became the only occupying force for Vietnam. Ho Chi Minh denounced the Japanese actions and declared they were Vietnam's number-one foe. Minh, an intelligent and pragmatic strategist, quickly realized that a major attack against the Japanese was futile.

First, he knew it wouldn't be successful against the Japanese who were better equipped, and second, he also knew that the full power of the Allied troops was nearly at their feet. Ho Chi Minh saw that the Japanese were getting ready for a last struggle with the Allies. Ho Chi Minh decided it was better to let the Japanese fight it out and sit back and observe the action unfold.

Ho Chi Minh created a controlled region of northwestern Vietnam with Viet Minh forces in June 1945, after the Japanese had been defeated. Ho Chi Minh's outpost was not a problem for the Japanese at that time, as they were fighting a death and life battle with the Allied troops.

While Japan turned its back against the Allies and Japan began to fight, the Viet Minh started to sweep down their northern base in order to retake Vietnamese settlements. At first they retook little villages, but as the battle progressed, they won more and better prizes. At the end August, Japan surrendered and the Viets Minh took control of the major Vietnamese cities of Hanoi & Saigon. The Viet Minh found themselves in a position of great importance to demonstrate that they were an independent power in Vietnam.

Ho Chi Minh declared on September 2, 1945 to the world that the Democratic Republic of Vietnam (DRV) had been created. Despite its aspirations of being the governing body in all Vietnam, "DRV", was merely an enclave to the north. With Japan's defeat, the British were actually the ones who would occupy South Vietnam.

Brits were also a weakening colonial strength at the end of World War II and had great sympathy for French interests. They sought to strengthen French claims. A joint British/French force arrived in the area that September. They discovered the land was in chaos and confusion. Although the Japanese government had acknowledged their surrender, the Japanese troops stationed on Vietnam's border were unable or unwilling to give up their arms.

It wasn't so much because we wanted to continue the losing fight for Imperial Japan but it was due the reality of life on the ground. Viet Minh constant harassment meant that the Japanese were unable to lay down their weapons, which would have led to certain death. They did not yet have an adequate withdrawal plan. So, to avoid getting shot in the back from Viet Minh Guerilla Fighters while trying an evacuation, they stood firm.

The British realised the suffering of the Japanese and allowed them arms to continue. Martial law was proclaimed, and the British were joined by the French and Japanese to bring the situation under control. By September 23, the communist fighters of guerrilla had been defeated and French colonial governance had been restored.

Chapter 4: France tries the Steering of the Tide

French troops, now back at power, did not forget about some insurgent Vietnamese and soon their anger led to drastic measures. French troops and civilians marched into Vietnam, arresting suspect Vietnamese. This treatment was met with a harsh response by the population.

The Viet Minh in the north were certainly not much better, since these communist agitators began killing anyone deemed to be counter-revolutionaries or collaborators with the French. As you can see the average Vietnamese citizen fell into a political trap, where they could be either targeted by the French administration or the Vietnamese communists.

Ho Chi Minh opened a dialogue between the French and Hanoi to demand that the DRV was recognized as Vietnam's sole government. The French refused, and continued to assert South Vietnam's claims.

The sides came to an agreement after more fighting and diplomatic back-and forth. This was in the spring 1946.

In the new agreement, France officially recognized the DRV (North Vietnam) in the French. French representatives in South Vietnam proposed holding an election to decide if South Vietnam should be united with North Vietnam or remain under French influence (if possible outright control)

Yes, France acknowledged the presence DRV in the North, but most hardline communists thought it was a travesty that France would not continue to be present in the South. Ho Chi Minh saw this as the best option at the moment, so he agreed to the terms.

Ho Chi Minh was able to consolidate his power by all this diplomatic wrangling. The French would quickly realize that the Viet Minh is a difficult foe and would need to be given more time. After much negotiation, talks were halted and an agreement was reached. The special conference between the parties was set for 1947.

The ceasefire was quickly broken by skirmishes involving Viet Minh soldiers and French colonials. These incidents escalated and the French finally took action. They took control the North Vietnamese city Haiphong. Ho Chi Minh maintained his options open, even though war seemed certain. He sought diplomatic dialogue and continued to seek out French help.

Ho Chi Minh gave his troops permission to start a new war when the last of these attempts failed. French forces responded by launching an aggressive assault against the north, in hopes of destroying Viet Minh strongholds located throughout the northern countryside. The Viet Minh excelled at hiding in hard terrain and were difficult for French forces to remove. French incursions were stubbornly repelled by pockets of resistance that were scattered and isolated.

However, what was most important for the North Vietnamese in this period was the establishment Viet Minh-run factories that could produce their guns and ammunition. The Viet Minh, having seen the French defeat their ancestors in the past and learned well from it, had decided to make their own guns and ammunition. They were determined not again to find themselves in this predicament.

Without this vital resource the Viet Minh could not have stood a chance. The French began to look for foreign assistance as the war continued into a bloody stalemate. Realizing that international support for arming was unlikely to be forthcoming, they began to search for diplomatic solutions. The French developed a plan known as the "Bao Dai resolution" and Bao Dai became a member to the Vietnamese royal dynasty.

French wanted this Vietnamese-born ruler to be in power.

Bao Dai was not a figurehead, through whom the French would take the final call. But it was hoped that at minimum a Vietnamese person would be added to the French's directives, which would provide some legitimacy. The United States for its part did not want to help the colonies fall, but fear of communism made it a compelling reason to support the French.

These ideological leanings grew stronger in January 1950, when the Soviet Union (China) and China (DRV) established official diplomatic relations. The whole communist bloc of Eastern Europe followed the example, with Yugoslavia recognizing North Vietnam's existence as a viable communist state.

Ho Chi Minh was given a boost by the words of acknowledgment. The Viet Minh then began to receive large amounts from communist nations in the form of arms and other goods. This incident, naturally, alarmed the United States. They officially recognized the French-controlled Bao Dai government that governs South Vietnam. Britain also supported France's Bao-Dai puppet government once the U.S. had sided with them.

The United States President Harry Truman sent $15 million in aid for the French puppet to make sure it could continue fighting against the communist North. This influx of cash, support and assistance allowed the French to initially make some inroads. The Viet Minh were defeated as the French retook strategic sites along the Mekong in the South. By 1952, most of the ground lost would be recovered by the French.

However, these achievements were contingent upon the support provided by the Vietnamese Nationalists. These were South Vietnamese local fighters that formed "Bao Dai's National Army", a group of militia leaders who had little love for Ho Chi Minh, communists or the Vietnamese. France's success rested on how well these troops were able to cohesion with France.

Because the French were distrustful of their troops, morale was already low. Soon enough there was infighting between French soldiers and Vietnamese officers that led to violence between the two sides. Viet Minh communists knew how to exploit this chaos. With more Vietnamese nationalists abandoning the French and the Viet Minh beginning to reestablish itself within the rural countryside in southern Vietnam,

Henri Navarre became the French's new commander in Vietnam. Navarre made the field more assertive. Navarre led daring raids against Viet Minh strongholds within the Red River Delta, during this time.

In response, the Vietnamese communists started a counter-operation within northwestern Vietnam. It led to a march upon the French possession in Laos. This was done in order to bring the French far into Viet Minh territory, hoping that they would outgrow themselves.

Navarre tried to head the VietMinh off at this pass by launching a large amount of French airborne troops over a valley called "Dien Bien Phu" near Laos. It is here that the Vietnamese, renowned for their hit-and runs tactics, decided it was time to fight openly.

The French believed that the hilly terrain would give the advantage to them against the approaching French. Thus, the strategy of an all out final confrontation with the French was created. This was the start of the climactic struggle. In March 1954, the Viet Minh launched a "human wave" attack in which hundreds of troops stormed into France to overwhelm them in waves.

This type war has a dramatic effect on its enemy, but it is one that can cost many lives. The Vietnamese had to quickly change tactics due to heavy losses. They dug deep into hillsides to find their positions and used their artillery for a pounding on the French. They were soon trapped and under heavy gunfire.

The defeat appeared certain so French representatives contacted Dwight Eisenhower (the U.S. President) to request military help. Eisenhower was not against intervention. He and his friends weighed the options. During brainstorming sessions, it was suggested to Eisenhower and his associates that a bombing campaign can be used to push the VietMinh back.

President Eisenhower failed to secure approval from Congress and the idea of U.S. Military Intervention was killed upon his arrival. Eisenhower refused the Congress's will and refused any executive action. The French lost the battle and were forced to admit defeat without any help.

Chapter 5: Holding Back the Communist North

French colonial ambitions regarding Vietnam were defeated at the Battle for Dien Bien Phu. Although the Viet Minh had won the battle, they were forced into accepting a partition of Vietnam. This would see the Democratic Republic of Vietnam control the north and Bao Dai the government in the south. Some communist hardliners were disappointed that the Viet Minh would agree to a complete country control, but China's pragmatic pressure won the day.

The Chinese were afraid that the Americans would intervene in Vietnam. The Americans had successfully repelled an invasion from North Korea during Korea War. They didn't want to see it happen again in Vietnam War. Ho Chi Minh wanted American intervention to stop a similar invasion from North Korea in the early 1950s. His forces weren't strong enough to withstand it.

Nonetheless, Ho Chi Minh stepped up his efforts to secure his position in Vietnam and strengthen the DRV Army over the following few years. He implemented a large-scale land reform agenda in 1955. This saw land being taken from wealthy landowners, and then redistributed among the poor peasants. While the landowners felt the impact of this reversal of fortune, the peasant community was bolstered and became even more loyal the DRV.

While all this was going on in North Vietnam, the United States wanted South Vietnam supported at all costs. Ngo Dinh Dien (the prime minister of South Vietnam) was at that point the prime minster. The United States tried to make him their ally by providing financial and military support.

Ngo Dinh Dien was unpopular. Ngo Dinh Dien was a dictatorial leader who resisted anyone opposing him. He led many unstoppable crackdowns in South Vietnam. The so-called "Denounce the Communists," campaign was one of his most notorious crackdowns. This was launched in 2005 and made a vast sweep of South Vietnam's rural areas to seize any subversives. This hardline policy against the communists would go awry and make many more sympathetic to them than the communists. This resentment led to the formation of the official communist rebel guerrilla troops of South Vietnam (the "Viet Cong") in late 1960. They were initially recognized as the "military branch" of the Vietnamese communists' "National Liberation Front." However, the group was really established underground in the late 1950's when Dien attempted to purge subversives.

This situation became worse when Dien in 1959 passed the "Public Law 10/59." This gave the authorities to jail or execute any person they felt was not loyal. The human nature of humans meant that corrupt officials quickly began to use these brutal measures to not only find subversives but also to frame rivals.

As soon as a corrupt crony made a claim against them for subversive conduct, everyone's life was at stake. It didn't take long for Diem's opposition to begin plotting his overthrow in the toxic sewer. It was November 2nd 1963 that Diem was slain by a military coup.

Durong V Minh replaced Diem as a general in the South Vietnamese military armed forces, the ARVN. (Army of the Republic of Vietnam). Later, it became clear that the American CIA supported this military coup. This regime shift was planned because Diem's hardline views were alienating the South, and a moderate leader like Durong Van minh would help to stop a collapse of South Vietnam government.

If this was indeed the plan of the CIA planners, they would discover that they were greatly mistaken. Because South

Vietnam's stability would increase after Diem was removed. Between 1963-1965, 12 South Vietnamese states were toppled in coup after coup.

It isn't clear if Diem died in a CIA approved manner or if it was a spontaneous reaction by the Vietnamese troops. Ironically, and unfortunately, it was only days before U.S. President John F. Kennedy approved Diem's overthrow. He, too, was hit by an Assassin's Bullet.

Lyndon Baines Johnson was the vice president of his administration and, as such, became the next American president. It became evident that the South Vietnam's unstable government succession could no longer hold the communists back by 1965.

President Johnson authorized the bombings of insurgents as part of a mission codenamed Operation Rolling Thunder.

In South Vietnam, the very first American soldiers were delivered just weeks after the bombing raid. Their number would soon rise to around 184 and 300 soldiers before the year ended. In 1967, the Rolling Thunder Campaign was over. It is estimated that an amazing 864,000 tons bombs had been dropped upon the North Vietnamese.

Despite American troops present on the ground as well as the continuous rain of missiles, the Viet Minh maintained their resolve to not only keep Vietnam at the seventeenth Parallel, but to conquer all of Vietnam.

The Vietnam War, Before 1968

Lyndon B. Johnson

The United States had been investing heavily in Vietnamese communism opposition for more than two decades. Looking back, the American war effort to defeat it in 1968 may seem like a fatal error. Even today, Americans find it difficult to understand how their leaders could have decided that such a course was in the nation's best interests. It is therefore important to begin to investigate how a succession American politicians, bureaucrats, military officers and military personnel managed to convince both themselves as well as the public that a communist Vietnam represented a serious threat for America's safety.

Vietnam's revolution came after months of violence, famine and chaos that followed World War II. Although the country had been an French colony since late 19th Century, the Japanese occupied the entire region shortly before World War II. Despite their pan Asian anticolonialism that they publicly supported, Japan did little to change the structure of political and financial control that the French had created.

Japan surrendered all its claims to its overseas empire and spontaneous revolts were started in Hanoi, Hue and the other Vietnamese cities. These were seized and proclaimed independent Democratic Republic of Vietnam (DRV), by the Vietnam Independence League (or Vietminh), on September 2, 1945. France, which had reoccupied the majority the country by the early 1946s, offered to grant the DRV limited autonomy in theory. However, the Vietminh rose to arms after the apparent limits of this autonomy became obvious. In the first instance of a long-standing trend, the French were able to maintain control of cities and the rebels held the land until the end.

Ho Chi Minh

Ho vowed to keep America at bay from the beginning. While he was a committed Communist, and devoted to class warfare and social revolution, he was also a staunch Vietnamese nationalist and was not willing to be a puppet of the Soviet Union and the People's Republic of China. Ho's real popularity in the country lay in his ability to tap into a long-standing popular tradition of resistance against powerful foreign Hegemons. It was a tradition originally directed at imperial China. As such, he made significant advances to Washington. He even used the American Declaration of Independence as his own declaration of Vietnamese independence.

The United States might not have objected to an independent communist DRV under different circumstances. Truman, Roosevelt and Truman had extolled Asia's independence and shown little respect for French colonial rulers. These subtle distinctions faded as Cold War tensions rose. After 1949, the Soviet Union increased their rhetorical and material support for Vietminh. In May 1949, Secretary Dean Acheson declared that Ho wasn't as nationalist or Commie. All Stalinists who live in colonial territories are nationalists . . Once they are in power, their objective automatically becomes subordination [of state] to Commie purpose." Young, 20 – 23.

Acheson

This led to the United States recognizing the new puppet government France under the emperor Bao Dai in 1950. American financial support funded over 60% of France's counterinsurgency effort by 1953. The 1954 failure of the effort led to an international conference at Geneva that agreed to split Vietnam at its 17th parallel between a communist DRV in northern Vietnam and an American-backed Republic of Vietnam south. Ngo Dinh Diem became the president of South Vietnam between 1955 and 1961. He received more than $1,000,000 in American aid. Despite the fact that Diem failed to secure support for his regime, he faced a rising insurgency with the Viet Cong. (VC), a coalition formed of local guerrilla bands supported by North Vietnam.

Diem

Bao Dai

American politicians and military leaders struggled with the tough question of how much sacrifice they were willing make to support an ally. Kennedy in 1961 refused to launch air strikes but agreed to increase financial aid for South Vietnam with hundreds, and eventually thousands, of American "military advisors."

Lyndon B. Johnson spent the summer 1964 working on domestic policy legislation. It was normally used to prepare for reelection. His efforts to accelerate domestic policy legislation were soon thwarted when a shocking foreign policy event occurred: the Gulf of Tonkin. In 1964, the USS Maddox was an intelligence-gathering naval ship stationed off the coast of North Vietnam for the purpose of gathering information about the ongoing conflict between North Vietnam and South Vietnam. However, North and South were at odds and the United States wasn't as updated on changes than the two other belligerents. The USS

Maddox accidentally crossed into North Vietnamese shores. North Vietnamese naval forces spotted the Maddox, and they attacked the Maddox the following day, August 2, 1964.

Despite the fact that no Americans were killed, naval crews were alerted as the Maddox moved to South Vietnam where it was met at the USS Turner Joy. Two days later, Turner Joy (and the Maddox) were sure they were being tracked by hostile North Vietnamese boats and fired at targets on their radar.

Johnson gave an address over radio to Americans shortly before midnight, August 4th, following the second encounter. Johnson told of the attacks on international waters and promised that the country would be prepared for the defense of itself and South Vietnamese. Johnson drafted and approved the Gulf of Tonkin Resolution. The resolution gave the President military readiness without the need to get approval from Congress. The resolution was adopted shortly thereafter. It gives the President the power to form military units in Vietnam, and engage in war if necessary without Congress' approval. Within a matter of minutes, President Johnson approved airstrikes on the North Vietnamese. Congress also approved military action under the Gulf of Tonkin Resolution.

Johnson once declared, "We're not about to send American boy 9 or 10 miles away from our home to do what Asian boys need to be doing for us." In South Vietnam, over 16,000 Americans were already stationed. Johnson would reply to Johnson that Johnson changed his mind and say, "Just like Alamo," somebody had to come to their aid. Oh, my God, I'm going for Vietnam's rescue!

It would be many years before the government admitted that the second encounter had not been a true encounter. Although Turner Joy was firing on the Maddox and Turner Joy at that moment, the government couldn't figure out the cause. However, there were no signs that it involved the North Vietnamese. Lyndon Johnson eventually agreed to Operation Rolling Thunder in 1965. He was under great pressure from his advisors. He also granted General William Westmoreland's request for the first American ground troops to Vietnam: two Marine battalions to guard the airbases.

Westmoreland

General Frederick Weyand speculated many years later that the disingenuous claims of politicians and officers may have poisoned support for long-term intervention. We believe that 'things'--artillery. Bombs. Massive firepower----are necessary to preserve the lives of our soldiers. The enemy on his part, however, was able to compensate for his lack 'things by using men instead of machinery and suffered immense casualties. The army witnessed the same thing in Korea. We should have made the facts of war more obvious to the American people, before they watched it on their TV screens. The army should make clear the price of participation before they get involved." (Summers.

While it is impossible for us to predict whether more openness in the beginning would translate into greater national resolve in the longer term, it would almost certainly have dispelled some of these dangerous illusions that American soldiers brought with them to Vietnam.

The average American soldier fighting in Vietnam was younger than the Korean soldiers who served before them. In World War II, an average American soldier was 26. In Vietnam, however, it was only 19. This could be partly explained by President Johnson's refusal not to mobilize the National Reserves. Johnson was afraid of alarming the public and provoking the Russians or Chinese. Instead, he relied upon the draft to fill his military ranks.

Between 1964-1973, nearly 2.2million Americans were drafted into the military. Additionally, an additional 8.7million enlisted voluntarily or at least semi-voluntarily. Men who expected to get drafted were aware that draftees would likely be assigned to combat positions. Many took the initiative to enlist before their chance was given by the Selective Service Board. This was a risky wager, but it wasn't impossible. Enlistees had a lower chance of being killed in Vietnam than draftees.

Additionally, due to the number of Selective Service Deferments available for those who are married or have a job in the defense industry, the burden of the draft fell heavily on people from working classes. It was particularly detrimental to African Americans.

These draftees and young enlistees fought in World War II. The resulting American military was temperated by two decades of

Cold War. In terms of its organization, equipment, training regimens, operational doctrines, and its very outlook, the American military was designed to fight a major conventional war against a similarly-constituted force, whether in Western Europe or among the plains of northeast Asia. The Army's collective memories include battles like the Battle of the Bulge at Incheon, Normandy (Iwo Jima), Midway, Normandy, Iwo Jima and Midway. These campaigns included battles of jet fighters and jet fighters. Many of those who fought in Vietnam as young men had played as soldiers growing up, reliving the heroic tales told by their grandfathers and dads. Philip Caputo - a young officer in the Marine Corps who arrived in Vietnam 1965 as a mariner - recalled "I could see myself charging up some distant beachhead, just like John Wayne in Sands of Iwo Jima, then returning home with medals upon my chest." (Caputo, 6).

American soldiers in their late teens, early twenties expected a simple conflict against evil, but they arrived in Vietnam unaware of the local culture. They found a world filled with peril, hardship, and moral uncertainty. Bruce Lawler, a CIA Case Officer in South Vietnam, expressed profound sorrow for Caputo and others, and he exploded with rage, "How in hell are you able to put people like this into a conflict?" How do you bring these types of guys into situations that require so much sophistication? You can't. The result is that they start shooting at all things because they aren't sure what they are doing. They're scared. I mean, they are out there getting shot at and Christ, there is someone with eyes different than mine. And boom! It's gone." Saltoli, 177.

Except for a few cases, American military experiences in Vietnam were mainly small-scale encounters. It was clear that participating in a conventional combative battle with the better-armed Americans was suicide. The Viet Cong waged an aggressive guerrilla campaign. This took advantage of their superior terrain knowledge, close relations with the local villagers, and their greater commitment to the cause. Viet Cong fighters didn't wear uniforms. They did not always show their arms, they did not adhere to traditional battle lines, and they blended in with the local villagers who supported them. An American soldier was equally likely to die from a landmine or boobytrap, or by a hidden sniper in wartime.

The VietCong believed that such tactics were natural and appropriate in a war against the "people". They said, "The soldiers come from the people." They were children of the villagers. They were loved by their village, and they fed, protected, and loved them. They were "the people's soldiers." [FitzGerald, 20]. However, Americans saw the insurgents as sneaky and treacherous. They were more inclined to hide behind women and children rather than fight like men.

However, such guerrilla tactics helped blur the lines between combatant & civilian. Specialist 4th Class Fred Widmer (Charlie Company) explained, "The exact same village you went into to provide them with medical treatment." . . It is possible to go through that village and get shot at by an sniper while you are on your escape. You wouldn't be able to find anyone if your back was turned. Nobody knew. . . "They were not trustworthy anymore," (Widmer).

General Westmoreland chose a war to attrition when faced with an opponent so determined, skilled in asymmetrical warfare, and enjoyed significant popular support. Although he did utilize strategic hamlets, peace programs, and other kinetic counterinsurgency operation, General Westmoreland opted to fight a war of attrition. He primarily relied on the huge advantage he had in firepower to take down the Viet Cong (South Vietnam's NVA). The goal of the operation was simple. It was to get to a point where communist fighters couldn't be replaced faster than they were killed. American ground forces would draw the enemy to the open where they could be destroyed with artillery or air strikes.

B-52 bombers, flying at upto 30,000ft, were extremely indiscriminate and could target entire villages, even though American soldiers had difficulty distinguishing civilians from combatants. American bombers and fighters-bombers in Vietnam had dropped around 825 tons of explosives per day by the end 1966. This was more bombs than were dropped on Europe during World War II. Robert McNamara (Secretary of Defense) wrote to President Johnson in May 1967, "The picture the world's largest superpower killing, or seriously injuring, 1,000 noncombatants each week, while trying hard to pound small backward nations into submission on an aspect whose merits and merits are hotly debated is not one that is attractive." Sheehan. 685

Since 1968, South Vietnam has seen a minimum of 300,000 civilian deaths per year. Westmoreland's brutal, yet ultimately ineffective, tactics have been widely criticized. Although he did have some options, it should be remembered that there were few real attractive alternatives. The Johnson administration had dismissed the idea of invading north to win a decisive victory. It was seen as too provocative as it could pull China or Soviet Union into World War II. However, Westmoreland had too few troops, too young and too inexperienced in order to wage a full counterinsurgency just like the British did in Malaya. Westmoreland later stated that "Had there been virtually unlimited manpower, I could've stationed troops permanently within every district or province, and so provided an alternative strategy." This would have allowed soldiers to get to understand the people and facilitate the task of identifying subversives. It also protected the rest from intimidation. That would have required literally thousands of men." Westmoreland.

It is possible that this is true. But it is hard not to admit that the strategy for attrition, and the vastly indiscriminate means used in achieving it, were bound to drive a wedge among the American military personnel and the anti-communist civilians. "Search & destroy" missions were meant to remove not only VC guerrillas from power but also any food and shelter that they may have used. Westmoreland, the Military Assistance Command, Vietnam, and (MACV), declared large swathes South Vietnam to be "free fire" areas. This meant that villages could be carpet-bombed and civilians could automatically become enemy combatants.

Most importantly, success was measured in terms "body count"; Westmoreland's team estimated the crossover at a kill to American ratio of 10 VietCong. Officers were rewarded for soldiers' confirmed kills. Rules were not enforced and operations were sometimes designed solely to increase body count. Philip Caputo noted that the results of such a strategy were just as predictable as the tragic ones for the American soldier. "General Westmoreland's strategy to attrition also had an important impact on our behavior. Our mission did not include capturing territory or seizing positions. It was simply to kill Communists. Stack them like cordwood. Victory was high body count, defeat low kill ratio, and war was an arithmetic matter. This pressure on unit commanders was so intense that they had to produce enemy dead bodies. They then relayed it to their troops. . . It is therefore not surprising that some individuals have developed a contempt towards human life and a tendency to take it." (Caputo. xix).

The Viet Cong's plans

A map of the targets for Tet Offensive

The Americans were not alone concerned about the 1967 impasse. Ho Chi Minh's war council discussed in Hanoi its own strategy for driving away the Americans and allies from south. 1966 was the year when the party agreed to pursue a "decisive triumph in a relatively limited time." (Duiker 263). But, aggressive battlefield operations involving both the Viet Cong guerrilla groups and the units of the North Vietnamese Army spirited to the south along the Ho Chi Minh Trail proved ineffective against the South Vietnamese Army's combined forces and the growing number of American troops in Military Assistance Command, Vietnam, MACV. One Communist general stated that "In the spring 1967 [MACV commander, General William] Westmoreland began the second campaign. It was very intense. Several people felt discouraged. There was much discussion about the war. Should we continue main force efforts or should our focus shift to a local strategy? However, by 1967, it was clear that South Vietnamese and Americans had not reverted the balance of forces on battlefield. So we decided that one decisive combat was necessary to force LBJ into de-escalation of the war." (Arnold, 9)

Le Duan, Secretary-General of the Lao Dong ("Vietnam Workers Party"), and General Nguyen Chu Thanh (head of the NVA's Central Office for South Vietnam), were both early advocates for this strategy. Le Duan attacked his more cautious companions, arguing for a surprise massive offensive that could strike both the Americans as well the South Vietnamese at their weakest: lukewarm public opinions in the United States and low morale within the South Vietnamese army establishment. Thanh expressed similar sentiments, arguing that a mass assault against South Vietnamese cities would set off a rebellion of discontented South Vietnamese civilians.

Le Duan

Nguyen Chi Thanh

It was interesting that Vo Nguyen Giap, North Vietnam's Defense minister, who would eventually organize the Tet Offensive (and is often credited with inventing it) actually opposed Thanh's proposal. Giap was in favor of a protracted, guerrilla fight against American supply and communications lines. He was worried that such large-scale guerrilla warfare would fail in the face American superior firepower and would severely reduce the war effort. Thanh ridiculed Giap as being old-fashioned. . . in accordance avec a dogmatic tendency." Currey (262 - 63)

Giap

After much debate, Thanh, Le Duan and the 13th Plenum voted in support of Resolution 13. It was a combined mass offensive and spontaneous uprising to win a decisive win in the shortest time. Thanh succumbed to a heart attack in July 1967. Giap was given the responsibility of planning the Tet Offensive and its execution, which he accepted despite personal reservations.

Giap's leadership outlined the Tet Offensive plan. It had three goals. The main ones were to destroy South Vietnamese military forces and incite civil unrest among South Vietnamese civilians. General Tran Vand Tra, Commander in South Vietnamese NVA Forces, stated that the Viet Cong sought to "breakdown and destroy the vast majority of South Vietnamese puppet [South Vietnamese] forces, topple any puppet administration at all level and take control of power; to destroy most U.S. force and their war matériel, and render it unable to fulfill its political and military obligations in Vietnam; break the U.S.will of aggression, force them to accept defeat and end all acts in war against the North." (Werner and Huynh).

Tra

It is worth noting how closely and completely political and militaristic goals intertwined in the above statement. Giap would later add, "For we, you will know that there isn't a single strategy." Ours is always one synthesis. It is simultaneously military and political as well as diplomatic. This is why the Tet Offensive has multiple objectives. (Karnow, 548). Giap never saw the Tet Offensive's ultimate goals as strictly military. He understood better than Thanh nor Le Duan that the North Vietnamese cause was doomed in a strictly combative war. Giap believed that military action was a way to change attitudes in South Vietnam as well as the United States.

Giap emphasized that the operation should use unprecedented reach and unprecedented shock in order to achieve these goals. Combined NVA/VC units would unleash a surprise attack on cities and military base in South Asia during the offensive. While previously unattemptened urban centers such as Saigon, Nha Trang and Qui Nhon, Quang Ngai and Hue were under siege, the American veneer of competence and control would be torn away. All Southern Vietnamese, including military officers and soldiers, would have to admit that nothing was beyond the reach and control of the VietCong.

The South Vietnamese military would have been caught unaware if the offensive was launched during the Tet holiday. Both sides had previously observed ceasefires during this period. In reality, the high level of travel and bustle during the holiday period would only serve to hide the torrents of materiel and men who were rushing into positions. In the weeks leading up Tet, VC operatives smuggled weapons & ammunition into the outskirts Southern towns in baskets of rice under truckloads and sometimes even in coffins. Northern troops disguised by civilians, or even Southern soldiers, were submerged in a sea of pilgrims who returned to their homes for the New Year.

Giap didn't just use passive surprise measures to win the Tet Offensive. He orchestrated a lengthy "preparatory period". From September to December 1967 Northern units struck repeatedly against isolated outposts in the hilly region along South Vietnam's Laotian or Cambodian borders. This large scale feint was meant to lure American and South Vietnamese forces west, away from densely-populated central towns and cities that would be the ultimate targets. These border strikes were not only confusing, but also diverted American attention away form the men and equipment infiltrating South Vietnam. It was also a great opportunity for NVA and VC soldiers to practice the urban streetfighting tactics that would play so heavily in their main offensive.

The Tet Offensive began with the Con Thien attack by NVA forces in July 1967. Con Thien is a Marine base located in the extreme northeast corner South Vietnam. The Marine battalion there endured artillery and ground attacks for three months. Finally, in spite of America's overwhelming air superiority (790 B52 sorties flown), NVA were forced from their position to lift the siege. They were forced to withdraw on October 31.

A map showing Con Thien's position in Vietnam

Con Thien was actually only the first of many border attacks. On October 27, a South Vietnamese battalion, located near the Cambodian border in Song Be, was attacked by an NVA-regime. And on October 29, a Viet Cong unit struck at a South Vietnamese military base at Loc Ninh. This is further south and west of the border. The first shots of a major confrontation occurred on November 17, when nine American and six NVA divisions fought for control over a U.S. Special Forces station near Dak To, in central Laotian highlands. These actions all had one thing in common: intense fighting, high casualties and a sudden attack.

During the border raids, American officers often expressed surprise over the tenacity of NVA and VC soldiers to support their positions. Prior to the Tet Offensive it was common to strike quickly, cause maximum damage and then disappear in the jungle before the South Vietnamese could respond with full force. However, the North Vietnamese used different tactics to seize territory in Con Thien. Song Be. Loc Ninh. and DakTo. These were tactics that would also be used during the main Tet Offensive. The border fighting was brutal and costly. Dak To, where 1,400 NVA soldiers were killed was an example. This compares to the deaths of about 350 Americans as well as South Vietnamese.

The Hill Fights

A map of the area

The Americans took Dien Bien Phu's lessons into consideration and developed a thoughtful approach to building Khe Sanh. Khe Sanh was situated in densely forested hill country. There was only one reliable route to the land, National Route 9 This narrow dirt highway ran through heavily vegetated terrain. It would be relatively simple to cut by a determined enemy. But it was just 28 mi away from the base and could be reached by military helicopters in 20 minutes.

A large number of French soldiers found themselves at Dien Bien Phu in 1954. This made resupply difficult, making it almost impossible even for the best of times. The Americans imagined a garrison smaller than 7,000 men. Large enough to defend itself, but small enough that it would be easier to supply with food, ammunition, or medical supplies.

American positions also showed the lessons of Dien Bien Phu. French had set up a single big base in a valley bordered by hills. This was the only thing they attempted to occupy. Viet Minh was able to take the hills and position their artillery in direct fire towards the French base. American outposts were built on the hills surrounding the Khe Sanh base. This allowed them to control the heights so that the NVA could not easily position guns near the US main position.

The final element, the massive 3,900 foot runway, served two purposes: it was both a supply station and could house aircraft used for recon operations or strikes on targets in Laos. General Westmoreland was impressed by the work of the MCB 10, the US Marine Engineering Battalion 10, in configuring and constructing the all-weather C-130 capable Khe Sanh airfield. There is no more important Vietnam Airfield from a tactical point of view [...] The construction of this airfield took place under extremely difficult circumstances, as the weather was very poor and the threat to enemy attack was ever present.

While the area was covered in NVA patrols, with their predictable small-scale raiding/skirmishing, it was not clear that the North Vietnamese had the numbers or the ability to significantly interfere. They failed to launch any operation against the airfield construction or base completion, despite the threats to the Ho Chi Minh Trail in Vietnam and North Vietnam.

Although the North Vietnamese did not manage to stop construction of the airfields they were able to occupy the hills north of Khe Sanh. The first meeting between the US Marines and the North Vietnamese was in January 1967. This series of battles is known as "the Hill Fights". They began in April 1967. The Marines took four critical hills named for their heights (Hill 881 South or 861S), Hill 558, Hill 558, Hill 950 and Hill 950 to protect the artillery of North Vietnam. They also moved towards clearing Hill 881

North or 881N. They almost immediately found out that NVA soldiers had dug into well-camouflaged underground bunkers and held several of the hills. The Leathernecks, eager to fight, advanced to dislodge their defenders.

A map of the hills

A photo showing Marines attacking Hill 0881N

A picture of fighting one of the hills

The Hill Fights began in April 1967. After some earlier clashes with the Khe Sanh hill country, it became deceptively tranquil for a while. Some soldiers described late March 1967 and early April 1967 like a vacation. While the Americans may have spotted NVA troops occasionally, the Vietnamese prefer to go away than engage. The Colt M-16 rifles first issue arrived during this peaceful time.

All of this changed when 2nd Platoon. Company B, 3rd Battalion. 3rd Marines moved for a mortar position on Hill 700. They set up their position beneath a dense cloud cover and received rain. Five Marines went to Hill 861 nearby. Lieutenant Philip Sauer led this small patrol. They were under AK47 fire as they climbed up the slope. Lieutenant Sauer bravely held firm to his position with the 1911.45 pistol he carried, trying to stop the retreat of the four patrol members. The high-velocity 7.62x39mm bullets from the NVA quickly struck his body and killed him. Other Vietnamese hid behind cover to pursue the four privates who fled, and all but Pfc were killed. William Marks. The rest of the platoon moved quickly to rescue the bodies after hearing Marks' gunfire. Hill 861 was quiet now, but they found American bodies naked on the hill. It felt almost like they were being observed. They returned with the bodies to Khe Sanh, where they received orders via radio.

Other elements of 3rd Battalion 3rd Marines explored Hill 861. They came under heavy attack from automatic weapons, likely with machine guns as well as AK47s. The NVA also used white-phosphorus grenades to inflict terrible and sometimes fatal wounds on many Marines.

The M-16 rifles which were issued to Marines during these conflicts often failed. Even though the M-16 is sometimes called a "Mattel-toy," it was an effective fighting weapon. Its earlier version, the M4 Carbine, proved itself to be a formidable combat weapon on many battlefields.

It was not evident to Marines in action, however. A soldier, unidentified, wrote about it in an open letter, which was read in Congress. [...] What did most of us die from? Our rifle. We were all given the M16 rifle before we left Okinawa. Practically every one was found with his rifle broken down right next to him. (Murphy, 2003: 296-297).

The actual fault was with the ammunition. The ammunition was not compatible with the rifle's recommended load. The M-16 operated with the same lethal reliability and accuracy of the AK-47's rifle, provided it had the right ammunition. However, the ammunition supplied produced massively greater chamber pressures, expanding the cases far too much for extraction.

Political maneuvering may have caused M-16 failures that claimed the lives of many Marines in their first major field usage of the rifle during Hill Fights. Influential procurement people felt the M14 provided greater utility due to its 7.62x51mm (7.308) cartridge. However trials accurately indicated that a 5 to 6-man section using M-16s in 5.56mm format offered the same firepower potential that 13 to 15 men with slower, less agile M14s.

James Sullivan and Eugene Stoner were part of the AR-15's design team. Robert Fremont was also a suspect in a scheme to sabotage

M-16s by issuing deadlyly inaccurate ammunition to try to persuade military personnel to keep the M-14. In a 2014 interview with Ian McCollum Sullivan, Sullivan said, "The final report – which was also the final report – was that the Army handled this in a way that was completely unbelievable and bordered criminal negligence." They couldn't locate anyone to blame. They could not prove that anyone had done it intentionally. But they did know what it looked. It was sabotaged. It was sabotaged.

The Marines did not know these things at the time. But it was evident that the newly delivered rifles failed them spectacularly. In reality, the NVA moved to the sound of signal whistlings due to the absence of any return fire. Some Vietnamese soldiers shouted English "Put in your helmets, Marines!" We're coming after you!" (Pisor, 1982, 13).

With no means of retaliation, the Leathernecks climbed back up Hill 861, leaving many dead on the slopes. Many of these corpses were found with cleaning rods in their arms, along with a fired chamber.

To save his battalion from destruction, he called for heavy airstrikes along with 155mm howitzer fires from nearby support firebases. F-4 Phantoms bombed the hill with 250-pound explosives, while B-52 Stratofortress fighter bombers dropped even heavier ordnance. Some bombs missed, resulting in friendly fire casualties. But the firepower slamming into Hill tore many NVA to pieces, forcing others to cease pursuit so that Marines could return to starting positions in relative safety.

A B-52 Stratofortress

The American commanders realized immediately that Khe Sanh was under Vietnamese control. They prepared for an aggressive operation to eliminate the enemy and establish American bases on these strategic eminences. The attacks were coordinated with bomber support, fighter-bomber support, and strong artillery.

3rd Platoon was able to capture an NVA deserter who had fled from his unit four day earlier. Bravo Company took him away the next day. Corporal Mike Brown relayed the story shortly after dawn. I wanted to run, because I thought they were surrounded. [...] And it turned to be just this young-looking Gook. He was shocked. He smiled. [...] Although he was carrying a cartridge belt and some ammo and demonstration equipment, he didn't have a rifle. We made him take everything off before he entered our perimeter."

Vu Van Tich, a deserter turned out to be an important smuggler. American intelligence believed his unit (the 32nd Regiment in the 341st District) was far from Khe Sanh. So his presence implied strong, secret NVA troop movements. Khe Sanh wouldn't be US intelligence without his desertion.

Over the next few days, the Americans attacked hills and eventually expelled the North Vietnamese. Aircraft provided bombing, napalm and support, while radio operators called up howitzer fire from the firebases. The Marines used machine guns, mortars, and recoilless weapons to defeat NVA resistance. Close air Support (CAS), in certain cases proved decisive, as one historian noted: [Hill 861] was also heavily covered with Napalm. On the first day, 75,000 pounds of fuel, approximately 10,000 gallons of jellied gasoline were delivered. All this was concentrated within [...] one-kilometer radius. It is not surprising then that 2/3, when it attacked Hill 861 on 28th September, found the objective, with its 25 bombers and more 400fighting holes, unoccupied" (Callahan, 2009: 47).

A picture showing the CAS bombing

Men had to storm the bunkers of other hills at melee range with rifles and guns, blowing in their doors using demolition charges. These strongpoints were dug by Vietnamese so deeply that even the most heavy American ammunition could not get rid of them.

However, the Marines successfully expelled the NVA out of the hills overlooking Khe Sanh. The Marines lost 155 and 700 men while clearing the hills. The Vietnamese lost 500 to nearly 1,000 men, while a large number were injured or evacuated. Because many Vietnamese died, many were buried in mass graves. It was difficult for us to know the exact number of those who died on the NVA. To the horror and disgust of the men involved in the incident, the Americans dug into the charnel mines while fortifying their hills.

The Marines were also given a warning by the Hill Fights. Random patrols stumbled upon NVA troops that were massed in readiness for a surprise attack at Khe Sanh. This alerted the entire American command hierarchy that occupying these hills should be a priority in defense of the base. Marines set up outposts along four of the most prominent eminences. This would prove crucial in the battle's outcome.

The Khe Sanh area became more peaceful and pleasant to visit during summer after the Hill Fights. The Americans set about building new bunkers and improving their fortifications. Also, they patrolled the rugged countryside. Ray Stubbe, the Marine Chaplain, recalls that it was an attractive place back then. It was in fact very beautiful. It was detached at the rear. We didn't get generals too often or people poking around. It was very cool to be high up the mountains. It was extremely colorful. It was alive with activity. It was well-respected by most people." (Steinman, 2002: 93).

However, this idyllic state of mind did not last past the dry seasons. September brought the monsoon showers, with many days of rain falling between 10 and 15. Khe Sanh felt extremely uncomfortable. Men were constantly cold, and they were covered in water for nearly 24 hours. Many of the bunkers had been built using earthen blocks and eventually collapsed. The packed dirt then became mud, making it difficult to reconstruct them. In addition to this, the airstrip began deteriorating, sometimes cutting off aerial resupply. This was possibly the most alarming change. An enemy attack could easily cut National Route 9 down, even if it wasn't impassible from mud. Marines used quarry crushed rock to rebuild the airstrip and made it more resistant to heavy monsoon floods.

In the same time, elements from the NVA moved into position to support the offensive. These men, unlike the Viet cong guerrillas that are used to jungle conditions found monsoon conditions much worse than the Americans.

The Americans had turned the base into a powerful modern stronghold before the Battle of Khe Sanh. It was surrounded by razorwire banks six feet high, creating a flesh-snagging barrier for any enemy who tried to gain entry. Aprons of barb wire, "tanglefoot," entanglements at calves height, chevrons, and other barbed wire meant funneling advancing foes to killing zones created a perilous maze. The Americans also planted lethal ordnance around the razor wire and barbed wire perimeter zones. Command-detonated Claymore mines were used, as well as many types of antipersonnelmines like the M16A1 Bouncing Betty. Based on the World War II German S-mine's design, it bounced to 4ft before detonating into shrapnel at a staggering 360deg.

Marines also installed antitankmines across specific routes, as if this wasn't enough. Many barbed wire and crates left behind conceal explosive booby traps. To make the infiltrating sapper/assault team easy targets for American defenses, tripwire flares were set up to wait for 30 minutes to shine on any tripwire flares. Similar, but limited, defenses protected hilltop positions.

The reconnaissance efforts to penetrate the dense forest surrounding Khe Sanh were almost as important than these wire barriers. These could be anything from simple patrols on foot or a continuous crisscrossing and collecting data by various types of aircraft. The US air force dropped sensors over large areas to make the American reconnaissance system more advanced. General Alfred Starbird saw the Muscle Shoals systems, which were a combination acoustic/seismic sensors. They were first used on the Ho Chi Minh track in the latter part of 1967. The ADSID's seismic sensors activated when there were four footsteps. Acoubouy transmitted actual sounds.

Starbird

A US Navy OP-2E Neptune, used for the MUSCLE HOALS System

Acoustic and seismic sensors were placed around Khe Sanh, by General Westmoreland, in January 1968. This occurred just before the start of the battle. The 21st Helicopter Squadron began dropping them from their Sikorsky CH-3 Sea King Helicopters. Soon enough, Navy, Army and Marine aircraft of many types joined in their efforts. Hundreds upon hundreds of sensors were placed on the ground and began transmitting data.

Khe Sanh was not able to detect all the objects in its sensor field, but it did provide some clues that were more useful than mocking American media reports and some historians who followed the media's lead. Natural scattering of automatic sensors from the air in rugged terrain with trees resulted instead in a neat pattern. However, Americans were able to create a database with sensor locations through triangulation and walking around the area looking for them. This allowed them to restore much of their sensor information's usefulness.

The sensors did not have infallibility. They could also return false positives. While natural sounds, animals, and glitches can all result in incorrect information being transmitted while humans might be unnoticed in some circumstances, it is possible for them to transmit false positives. They provided an additional source for information. This reading reached the underside of the forest canopy. American detection efforts were greatly enhanced if they were used properly. This was especially true in rainy and dark areas, as well as remote areas of Khe Sanh.

As a final point in intelligence gathering, the Americans paid great attention to elephants. The NVA used large pachyderms to transport heavy equipment in the densely forested areas. Any elephant sign could be a warning sign that there was an imminent major attack in Khe Sanh. This is why foot patrols looked out for elephantdung and pilots flew close to any elephants seen openly. The red-bellied or pink-colored elephants could have been brought down the Ho Chi Minh Trail from Laos by their reddish or mud undersides. Gray-bellied eagles probably hailed originally from Khe Sanh, which was home to around 2,000 wild elephants in the country. Fred Locke was one of the pilots who expressed his amazement at seeing NVA-emaciated elephants from above. It's Lost Weekend, I know. They were the 'pink Elephants'. But there they were. (Prados, 1991,66).

Despite all the efforts of radar scans, sensors, radar scans, and aerial reconnaissance, the North Vietnamese are still elusive. The Americans were able determine the general activity of the area and even make guesses as to whether it has been increasing or decreasing. NVA sightings were rare until the Battle.

The Battle Starts

A map of the lines, January 1968

A photograph taken from above of Khe Sanh's perimeter

In the early days of 1968, a single but alarming incident alerted the 26th Marines' Commanding Officer, Colonel David Lownds as well his men and superiors about an imminent attack upon Khe Sanh. On January 2, 1968, a listening device with a dog and its companion reported that human intruders were nearby. Lieutenant Nile Buffington and Captain Richard Camp sent out a team to investigate.

The dark night outside Khe Sanh was pitch black, and the adhoc units spread out to form a line. They then moved into the night. Marine mortars fired starsills to illuminate the ground ahead of them as they advanced. The yellowish white glare revealed six men dressed in black pajamas (or military uniforms) depending on which account. Lieutenant Buffington yelled for assistance. However, he was not answered by the Marines who opened fire on them, mowing them to death. The Marines returned from the attack due to the darkness outside of the starshells' range. They waited for the morning to return to base. Captain Richard Camp, who monitored NVA radio communications with FOB-3's night crew, heard a loud explosion of frantic radio messages approximately one hour after Marines had shot six NVA. After a while this was gone again.

Captain Camp and Lieutenant Buffington returned early on the morning January 3, to find the remains of five North Vietnamese, one being extremely tall, at the scene. While searching for survivors of the attack, they found that one had taken off the uniform shoulder boards as well as other rank insignia. This indicates that all the bodies of dead men must have been officers, or at least high-ranking ones. A map case was also found amongst the bodies. After removing the insignia and retrieving documents and maps from the cache, the last survivor of six-man group crawled to a nearby treeline, less than 60 meters away. After being severely wounded, he left a clear track of blood and was located almost immediately by the Marines. Max Friedlander (Gunnery Sergeant) recounts that he began walking in the direction of a German shepherd's leash and eventually came to a wooded area. I didn't see anything and lost the trail so I walked further. I was already about sixty yards from their bodies. I saw a large, red log just to my right, at the treeline. I stopped, looked around and walked back to where everybody was. "I found out that there was an NVA company in the treeline. They were ready to open fire upon me and the Marines if I continued my walk." (Hammel. 1989, 21).

The Marines did not know of the assault rifles or machine guns that were trained on them in the green verge forest so they retrieved the bodies from Khe Sanh. The Americans took the long, presumably Chinese corpse to Phu Bai for further examination. Doctors and the 17th Interrogation-Translation Team (ITT) inspected the others at Khe Sanh, taking plaster casts of their faces. They were also carrying pistols and belt buckles made of gold or silver, rather than the standard NVA aluminium buckles.

In no time, the Americans arrived at the unmistakable conclusion that the five NVAs killed were evidence of an officer reconnaissance. As signs of enemy activity rose sharply, high-ranking Marine officers only approached the objective immediately before a major assault. Large numbers of footprints began appearing in the forest's soft earth, and North Vietnamese started ambushing Marine patrols with their weapons, killing a few.

Two divisions under Tran Quy Hi and Le Quang Dao the political commissar had sent support artillery and mortars to the area in December. The Vietnamese had built up supplies to sustain this force, and for the planned Tet Offensive.

Tran Quy Hai

General Westmoreland authorized the detailed planning of Operation Niagara in January 2005, knowing that North Vietnamese troops would soon be attacking Khe Sanh. Operation Niagara included a large-scale, continuous airlifting of supplies to Khe Sanh Base to ensure that it was operational after the enemy cut National Route 9 in half. Khe Sanh is not able to defend this narrow, forest-fringed dirt route so any assault on Khe Sanh will likely include blocking all overland supplies. Also included was close air support via fighter aircraft, bombers, or helicopters. Westmoreland explained: "The probable buildup enemy forces around the western DMZ gives us an opportunity to plan a comprehensive information collection effort and coordinate B52 and tactical aircraft strikes. We should be ready for surprise attacks and disruptions of enemy plans to launch an offensive [...] via heavy bombing on a consistent basis." (Rottman. 2005: 54).

A picture of supplies being flown to Khe Sanh

Following President Johnson's statement, "any damn Dinbinphoo" was not what he wanted (Dien Bien Phu), Marines maintained high alert right through January 1968. Further reinforcements arrived. The Marines increased their position and stockpiles increased. Scouting continued in all forms to collect information.

On January 20, a single NVA appeared east of the runway, carrying a small white flag tied to the barrel his AK-47. Bravo Company's 2nd Platoon of Captain Kenneth Pipes was there to greet him. Marines advanced towards the tiny, unclothed figure wearing khaki and supported by an M-50 Ontos. Strangely, the Ontos, which moved on tracks like tanks, but only 9 1/2 ton, was able to carry three 106mm reloadable rifles and was small enough that it could be seen from the turret. The Ontos protruded forward as if it were an ancient beast's antlers. Although it was lightly armored by Marines, they loved the vehicle. The Vietnamese however feared its effectiveness.

The man wearing the white banner showed no fear for the Americans and their vehicle. He surrendered right away and the Leathernecks brought Max Friedlander to question him. Friedlander was shocked to learn that the deserter was Lieutenant La Thanh Tonc. He accepted a meal and smoked some American cigarettes. Tonc spoke easily and openly to his captors. Friedlander explained that Tonc spoke openly to his captors as he was eating and talked about his families. He was married and had many kids. He was extremely disillusioned, especially when it came to politics. [...] Clearly, he wasn't a believer in the cause he had been fighting. [...] Disgruntled that he wasn't promoted, he complained. The man was very nice to me. I was sorry for his family [...]. Before he finished, he asked me if I could get him a radio music channel up north. He enjoyed it tremendously, so I did. It was the first time that he'd heard music in a while." (Hammel. 1989,57).

Tonc explained to Friedlander, following his meal, the plans for an attack against Khe Sanh that very evening. These included surround and isolating Hill 801S, as well attacking Hill 861 together with a sapper unit. Following the seize of Hill 861 by Marines, three NVA battalions would make their way through the Marine defenses. Artillery as well as rocket fire would attack the base simultaneously to cover the assault. One mortar force would close the Marines' Hill 950 base, while another mortar fire would destroy Khe Sanh's ground helicopters and attempt to eliminate them.

Friedlander took down his notes and ran from the interrogation chamber straight to Colonel Lownds' Headquarters. Staff Sergeant James Brown remained to complete Tonc's briefing. Lownds reviewed Friedlander's reports and sent him to Lang Vei by helicopter to report on Lownds. From there, the information quickly got to 3rd MarineHQ in Phu Bai and then finally to General Westmoreland at Saigon. Friedlander returned from Khe Sanh to board another helicopter.

Tonc continued to elaborate on other elements in the North Vietnamese plan. Some units would build antiaircraft weaponry and shoot down helicopters coming towards Khe Sânh's aid. Other mortar batteries could strike other targets within the base. Lownds had already raised alert levels and ordered that all Marines wear flak jackets, helmets, and other protective gear at all times. Additional security measures included requiring half of all units to remain alert during the night and removing units that were engaged in skirmishing between Vietnamese elements to the hilltop.

NVA 325C Division attacked Hill 861 with their first attack shortly after midnight. It had dug up Hill 881N along with the hills around it. Sappers crawled over the wire trying to cut the wire. The Marines from Kilo Company (3rd Battalion), 26th Marines (3/26) fired at them. The Leathernecks were able to hear the NVA talking and laughing between themselves during the grenade shots. It was a surreal scene that served as psychological warfare.

Two red signal beacons shot up in the dark and foggy sky minutes later. After several seconds, a torrent of artillery and mortar shells as well as rockets pounded Kilo Company on Hill 861. Despite thick, misty darkness, most American bunkers were destroyed by the NVA using a preplanned fire plan. As the barrage continued, fires from an automatic weapon system originating approximately 30 feet up than Hill 861 cut through the position. Marines responded using.50 caliber machine weapons and 106mm Recoilless Rifles. Their 60mm mortars decimated the NVA positions. However, their heavier 81mm mortars could not be heard and had no ammunition. Kilo Company's command point was destroyed by an incoming shell. It also severely wounded Captain Norman Jasper, and killed other men. Kilo Company's First Sergeant Stephen Goddard was a highly experienced Marine that Kilo Company relied on. A NVA machinegun bullet hit his neck. Goddard grimly clamped on to the artery until it could be closed between his fingers. He would survive.

First Lieutenant Jerry Saulsberry was the Marines' first lieutenant. The Marines kept firing while facing the mortar barrage. The NVA lifted their barrage but cleverly instructed sappers to place sticks of Dynamite over the wire in order to simulate mortar shell explosions. The ruse worked. Marines kept cover, while NVA soldiers moved forward and struck the northern end. 1st Platoon remained on the ground.

Realizing that the assault was beginning in earnest the Leathernecks demanded starshells. Michael Stahl described what happened: "Hundreds and thousands of NVA were climbing up our hill, along the slopes. They were shouting, firing. It looked very much like a football field, with the spectators watching from the air." (Prados, 1991, 246)

Hill 881S was not under attack despite Tonc's claims. The 60mm mortar, 81mm mortar, and mortar crews of India Company opened fire supporting Kilo Company on Hill

861. NVA was defeated by 680 mortar shots from the second hills. FOB-3's radio monitors were able to listen in real time as the commander of the attacking force tried for hours to have his reserves released by his superiors. They never arrived, and the officer's voice escalated to a panicked scream of frustration before finally stopping.

Marines battled with determination and professionalism, despite heavy attacks that continued into the early hours of the morning. To keep their morale up, the Marines started singing the Marine Hymn more often later in the night. The sound of voices rose among the sounds of shells, machine guns and automated rifles rattle, the sharp screams that charged NVA and the moans the dying.

"First to stand up for liberty and right."

And to keep our honor pure,

We are proud and honored to hold the title

United States Marine."

A green flare appeared at 6:30 a.m. as the sky was getting darker. Hill 861 became quiet as the NVA disintegrated. Marines discovered 45 bodies on the slopes, along with extremely large blood trails. There were hundreds more rifles and equipment left on the slope. After a few days, the smell of corpses and other equipment grew so strong that some men had to use gas masks as they held the line. Only four Marines lost their lives in the fight. Another 30 were injured.

Khe Sanh was the victim of heavy mortar and artillery bombardment that fell on it during the assaults on Hill 861. The sound of incoming mortar shells, their thunderous, loud explosions and brilliant orange flashes shattered the night's relative quiet. An ear-shattering detonation decimated any smaller explosions in just a few seconds. An NVA missile struck the 1,500-ton Main Ammunition Depot at the east side of the base and sent it high. Secondary explosions caused destruction to the burned dump, scattering wreckage as well as dangerously unexploded weapons across the entire compound. However, Marines still had easy access to a secondary dump on the opposite side of the base. They also had caches nearby each of their guns and they reacted vigorously.

A picture taken during the battle of the fuel dump

NVA units attacked NVA-held hills in the North, while others launched an attack against Khe Sanh village, three kilometres to the southwest from the fortified bases. Captain Bruce Clarke, 175 men including some South Vietnamese soldiers of the 915th Regional Force and Americans, held the hill overlooking village. Thick vegetation grew all the way to the wire. The fog that rolled in on the night Jan 20-21 actually served the defenders' benefit. The NVA forces sent to Khe Sanh village were caught in fog and plodded along for a while. Clarke, his men, and the enormous explosion of the ammo dumped put Clarke on full alert. Only 30 minutes later did Clarke finally start to panic.

George Amos wrote his wife a letter in which he described the beginning of the attack. [...] at the beginning of the attack, our compound was receiving incoming mortar rounds in the 82 mm format. We slept through them till about 4:45. Jim (Taronji), who was my tentmate, awoke to find out what was happening. He came running back into the tent and told me to "Get to that bunker, we are under attack." I ran out of my bed to get to the cement bunker assigned to me. I later found unexploded mortar a few feet from my tent. (God is my God!) At precisely 5 AM, the NVA attacked. We fired everything at them and they kept coming." (Clarke. 2007, 53).

Under the fog, the NVA worked close and at distances of less 50 feet. The Americans, on the other hand, used the pagoda to light heavy fire. The Americans managed to keep their compatriots in contact, but were unable see anything. Captain Clarke called out artillery fire directly from his own position in response to the Vietnamese rising pressure. The howitzers emitted shells fused for a burst, dumping a metal hail of shrapnel onto the ground. The NVA, however, had no shelter from this fire because of the NVA's bunkers. Most of them were very young. They grouped together in the darkness as a reassurance, and the shrapnel pulverized whole families together.

The NVA continued to apply pressure on the village throughout the day. The fog didn't recede, providing them with cover to check the Marine defenses. Although they were temporarily forced back by noon airstrikes, they did not retreat too far. Marines sent from Khe Sanh to reinforce the outpost ran out on the way of continuous firefights and had to return home. The defenders did gain support, however. Overflying helicopter crews retrieved crates with ammunition for them.

Marines in Khe Sanh village stopped some of the flames from the concrete pagoda. The Marines pounded its walls with LAW fire, which eventually put out the rest of the NVA sappers. Captain Clarke stopped NVA Sappers trying to penetrate the wire defenses via explosives. Clarke shot a M79 grenade launcher at the lead sapper and cut it in half. NVA bombardment at the main bases continued.

Clarke's little force was being reinforced by the Americans at the end of the day. Quang Tri was home to 10 UH-1 Huey Helicopters. The rotorcraft was piloted and crewed in America by Americans. 50 ARVN were carried by the 256th Regional Force Company. The helicopters could also carry supplies, 5 gallon water cans, as well as several tons of ammunition. Clarke's main address was not reached by the helicopters.

The Americans were unaware that the 11th Company (NVA 66th Regiment)'s 9th Battalion was concealed nearby, waiting for an opportunity. Tran Di Ky, their commander kept them in line until the helicopters began landing. The NVA opened fire with machine gunners, RPGs and antitank guns. The first ARVN troops to fall on the ground were hit with a hailof bullets. Tran Dinh Ky, Captain Thomas Stiner's pilot, fired a B-40 Antitank Rocket at Tran Dinh Ky as he attempted takeoff. The rocket hit the helicopter and set fire to it. It sent it plunging down the hillslope above the Old French Fort. Lieutenant Colonel Joseph Seymoe (a crewman) was killed instantly. A portion of the wreckage had also been set on fire, leaving him pinned underneath it. Stiner escaped, but he would be captured by Marine patrols as a Russian adviser. Tran Di Ky would become a decorated North Vietnam war hero and would eventually escape.

NVA had fired prematurely on the relief force, killing only a small portion of the ARVN group. However, they had forced the abortion of the mission. Clarke and his men remained isolated and were shelled heavily by NVA guns and harassed snipers. Clarke "walked", periodically, curtains of artillery assistance over the approaches on January 21-22. Douglas AC-47 'Spooky' gunships dropped flares as a way to make possible attacks.

NVAs around Khe Sanh village were melted by bright, sunny January 22. They left behind scores and fragments if corpses as well as blood trails showing where many of their victims were killed or wounded. Marines seized over 100 discarded weapons including an AK74 assault rifle, which one later claimed was a Marines weapon. This was impossible at the moment so it was more likely that it was a Czech-made VZ-58. SFC James Perry reported: "We went into the village looking for our Vietnamese counterparts. They were gone. We were treated like heroes by the villagers. It was incredible! There were many enemy bodies around our small camp. I counted 40 dead bodies, and took 2 rolls. Plus equipment and parts from bodies. The barbed wire had a hand- and arm hanging off it (took photos).

The losses to the Marine, South Vietnamese, Bru Montagnards in the fight against Khe Sanh village amounted 11 killed and 29, while the NVA sustained an estimated 1,000 casualties due to artillery supports and airstrikes.

The fighting capabilities of 66th Regiment were hampered by the small outpost. However, ammunition was running low after the destruction and re-supply of the main ammo repository. Lownds told Clarke that he could stop supporting Khe Sanh village with artillery. Reluctantly, the Marines boarded helicopters and returned the main Khe Sanh Base to their base. The Vietnamese villagers fearing reprisal from communists abandoned the village. They reached Khe Sanh five miles away. The Americans flew them all to the coast on January 23.

The NVA effectively drove the Americans from Khe Sanh village. However, this effort was so costly that it was not worth it to their commanders.

The Siege of Jerusalem

Khe Sanh village was taken by NVA. However, the attack on Hill 861 proved to be a fatal failure. The North Vietnamese established a siege. Americans continued their efforts to improve their position, as well as strengthening against any future attacks. Ammunition Supply Point 1 ("ASP-1") had been destroyed so ammunition became a top priority to resupply. Fairchild C-123 Provider transport airplanes were forced to fly in the dark of the night to avoid the impact of the storm of fire on Khe Sanh. The aerial resupply link landed 120 tonnes more after daylight made flights safer. This was just a few short hours later on January 21.

American media was already disillusioned by war's course and painted Khe Sanh battle as a disaster. Publications carried a picture showing an explosion in the ammo dump on the front pages for weeks. In addition, journalists made much of President Johnson's frightening (and inaccurately stated!) statement that a Nuclear Weapon might be necessary to stop NVA. To portray the Marines almost defeated, they used the image. For example, The New Republic claimed that the situation could end in a "military disaster" like the Vietnam War. Life magazine spoke of a "looming massacre at Khe Sanh" (ibid., 38).

Indeed, Colonel David Lownds (and his superiors) took strong steps, some of which were quite aggressive to improve the tactical position in favor the Marines. While NVA bombs and rockets continued falling on the base, the Marines took action to repair the damage, strengthen bunkers and fortify gun positions further.

Alpha Company of the 1/26 Marines joined Kilo Company at Hill 861 on January 21st. The Echo Company of 2/26 was then able to occupy Hill 861-A, the higher ridge from where the NVA had swept through 861 with machine gunfire. 1,200 men were present when the 1st Battalion 9th Marines (1/9) arrived at Khe Sanh via helicopter. They occupied Rock Quarry to guard Hill 861's flanks and resupplylines from the base. To further strengthen their formidable hill positions, several companies constructed new outposts.

While the Marines responded strongly to the attacks by improving its position, NVA did not remain idle. Marines limited their patrols to 500 meters from the base due to heavy patrolling and skirmishing.

The BV3333rd Laotian Royal Battalion arrived on Lang Vei Special Forces Base at 3:00 p.m. The 500 soldiers and the 2,200 civil refugees that followed them were in complete chaos when they reported a NVA PT76 tanks attack just a few kilometers inside Laos. The 33rd Royal Laotians were attacked by a large contingent of infantry and defeated in a short time by the Soviet light amphibious Soviet Tanks.

American pilots responded to this information and sent aircraft to destroy the bridge. Seven PT-76 tanks were spotted and attacked by American pilots. The South Vietnamese government introduced NVA armor for the first time. However, the Green Berets stationed here at Lang Vei were suspicious of the Laotians, as they believed their weapons had been used in desperate battles. They first disarmed the soldiers. However, Lieutenant Colonel Soulang was the leader of the unit and convinced the Americans not to take their guns back.

Instead, the Laotians created a defensive position in a Green Beret camp half-mile north.

The NVA's role was to only skirmish and bombard the Khe Sanh Base with rockets. Because the Marines had taken over the hills nearer to their base, they fired rockets and artillery at a considerable distance. Although they did less damage than they could, it left the men on edge.

Khe Sanh welcomed the ARVN 37th Ranger Battalion, which arrived on January 27. Hoang Pho commanding, the men took up positions near the end of Khe Sanh's airfield. Hoang Pho proved a bit of an entrepreneur, initiating raids against NVA himself. This included the capture of a 37mm Recoilless rifle and the destruction and dismantling of a North Vietnamese mortar fire battery.

A few days later and while the Marines were still hunkered down in Khe Sanh's vicinity, the Tet Offensive began throughout

Vietnam on January 30-31st 1968 during New Year celebrations. Curiously though, Khe Sanh itself saw that the North Vietnamese respected and followed the Tet truce. They didn't surprise attack to break it. Six mortar shells were dropped inside American defenses. But, the peaceful silence that followed fell upon the landscape and the NVA guns ceased to be heard on January 30. While the Americans used heavy B52 strikes to target areas near the base where there were likely assault forces, all evidence suggests the NVA that was surrounding Khe Sanh actually stood down for the Tet holiday.

The shell-pocked hilltop base and hills that commanded it were not able to keep peace. The electronic ADSID devices and other high tech gadgets found scattered through the forest proved their worth the night of Feb 5. The "Muscle Shoals" sensors began to track the movement of many living beings west of Hills 881S-861S and 861A at dusk.

Therefore, Marines conducted a sudden torrent artillery fire mission against the precise coordinates given by the sensors. NVA soldiers were gathered at their jumping-off points by a torrent of shells. Marines could then listen in to the results thanks the listening devices. Kenneth Houghton, the leader of III MAF intelligence section and Kenneth Houghton were among those who took advantage of their front-row seats. Dave Lownds has immediate access to the CP [command post]. We can hear people moving. We hear the screams when we fire artillery. It's breathtaking. It's music. They are really heart-curdling. We can pick up tracks. We can also tell if the artillery is tanks. It's so great." (Prados, 1991, 302.

Between the sound of artillery fire hitting the NVA troops, the intelligence officers heard many screams. They also heard panicked flight from the survivors, who ran back past the listening equipment. An estimated 2,000 NVA soldiers assembled for the attack. However, an unknown number perished when American artillery struck them suddenly from the night skies.

The sensors failed detect one NVA regiment moving against Hill 861A. This is the ridge where Echo Company 2/26th held Hill 861. The men only had time for parting out their defenses. They had just enough time to put five strands on their perimeter and dig weapons pits. They had already built some bunkers but hadn't finished reinforcing them.

Watchmen at Hill 861-A noticed that the fog was so dense that they could not see the edge of their wire. Then, suddenly, a strange and intense smell washed over the Marines. Some said it smelled similar to the sweat of many men who have not been bathed in a very long while. Others thought it was some type of drug. As a massive mortar barrage from several NVA mortar units suddenly crashed into Marine positions on Hill 862-A, they were soon able to find the answer. The mortar fire was directed at specific gun bunkers and pits. This indicated that NVA mortar crews had prepared a fire plan. The relatively weak wire defenses were attacked by Sappers who used Bangalore torpedoes. A section of pipe, or specially made metal tubing, filled with explosives was used to blow lanes. NVA attacked immediately with a battalion-sized division.

The 1st Platoon, Easy Company commander Lieutenant Edmund Shanley, had been held back by trenches. They were overthrown by their determined attack. However, the NVA soldiers behaved in a way that suggested that drugging might not be so farfetched. Many of them ran backwards, throwing bombs into the bunkers and while laughing and giggling loudly. Many of them, instead of pushing the attack on the Marines, stopped to loot them or their positions. Others even sat in groups to inspect the photographs of naked women in captured Playboy magazine and similar publications.

NVA troops put enough pressure onto the Marines, whether they were drunk or actually on drugs, to encourage their enemies to rally. Marine mortar teams dropped their range to zero and pitched shells into their trenches. Some suffered minor injuries from bits of their own shrapnel.

Captain Earle Breeding led the counterattack by leading a group Marines. Breeding's Marines rushed into the victory lane and began to fire grenades at their adversaries. The NVA soldiers then closed in and began attacking their opponents with bayonets. The NVA soldiers didn't have the stomach to fight in this melee, so they fled in terror and left the hilltop no more than 30 minutes after their attack started. Hill 558 had recoilless rifles that enfiladed the NVA's retreating position. They fired antipersonnel flechettes rounds at the NVA, while Echo Company's mortar crews launched a fast barrage on the NVA from nearby hills. The NVA launched only a weak attack at 6:10 a.m. but was quickly stopped by mortar and M60-type machine gun fire. American casualties were zero during the second assault.

Marines lost seven Marines and 35 were severely wounded in battle. Captain Breeding forbade his men from leaving the perimeter to count dead soldiers further away, fearing ambush. This resulted in a minimum death toll of 109 NVA troops. The NVA, apparently outraged by their failure to attack, shelled the hill heavily over the next day. Khe Sanh itself was also bombarded temporarily. Helicopter reinforcements arrived on Hill 861-A to replace Marine casualties.

The Final Stages

The NVA turned its attention to Lang Vei instead, an outpost located west of Khe

Sanh after they were thwarted in their attempt to take the hills to Khe Sanh's northwest. It was held by Green Berets (33rd Royal Laotians) The outpost housed men as well as a large collection of mortars and several recoilless weapons, as well dozens of machine guns and ammunition. The outpost was held hostage by Captain Frank Willoughby, an American.

NVA PT-76 amphibious vehicles rolled through Lang Vei at 12:15 a.m. The armored vehicles traveled through Laos to reach Lang Vei. American aircraft avoided them by not following the main tracks or roads. Instead, they "swam," for miles along rivers and used narrow forested tracks to get around detection. The Green Berets did manage to kill two PT-76s while setting fire to them with rounds from their 106mm reloading rifles. With several flechette "beehive" round, they also fired at NVA support infantry. A third PT-76 suffered between five- and six hits with light-antitank weapons, despite its fragile armor. Marines later discovered the vehicle's unusual design of mostly empty compartments made it difficult for the LAW to penetrate. Other LAWs did not work.

Pictures of disabled PT76 tanks

Despite fierce resistance and artillery and aerial strikes, the NVA rapidly overran Green Beret camp. Willoughby radioed Khe Sanh to ask for a prearranged rescue force. It had, up until that point, been part Lang Vei defense plans. Lownds however refused to send Marines into the Green Berets aid believing it was a suicide mission. He had in hand reconnaissance photos of the NVA creating an ambush location on Route 9 that was between Khe Sanh (and Lang Vei) several days ago.

While the Green Berets, which survived, retreated deep within their bunkers, NVA tanks and soldiers moved freely inside the wire. Eight Americans crowded in the command bunker along with a number of Bru Montagnard Fighters and a contingent of South Vietnamese Rangers. Others Americans and rangers fled the scene under darkness to the 33rd Royal Laotians. However, they were still holding on with 500 men in Old Lang Vei camp.

After dawn, NVA had succeeded in tearing down one wall in the bunker. A translator called down in English, asking that the occupants yield. The Green Berets attempted to defy the order, but the Montagnards or Vietnamese rangers refused and surrendered. Their choices were not well-made. They were all taken into NVA custody and never made it back to their homes.

Willoughby sent in an airstrike to provide cover. The 8 Americans, most of whom were severely wounded, made a desperate run towards Old Lang Vei. They were able to bring down the NVA sufficiently that the wounded made a slow, limping dash through the open. After killing the NVA's machine gun team, they discovered a truck driven to them by Lieutenant Quy of South Vietnamese Special Forces. Quy drove swiftly to Old Lang Vei where the men were able crawl into the truck's bed.

Two helicopter sorties out of Khe Sanh were supported by helicopter gunships. They airlifted the Americans as well as the South Vietnamese and Laotians with serious injuries. Despite their heroic efforts to climb onto the rescue helicopters for help, the uninjured Laotians were left behind. They were angry and frustrated at being left behind and fired at the departing Rotorcraft.

Colonel Soulang from the 33rd Royal Laotians advised his men to divide into small groups so that they could cross into Laos or travel to Khe Sanh, depending on their preferences. The Laotians dispersed, and they evaded. Soulang decided to go the Khe Sanh way. He was joined by 74 soldiers as they reached the base perimeter. Marines disarmed them then placed them in an enclosed shell crater.

Soulang and his men received their weapons back that day. Soulang then received food and access to showers. Lownds turned down many of the villagers who showed up at Khe Sanh. They were afraid of infiltrators and refused them admission. Many of the villagers walked around base and then turned east.

With Khe Sanh's western approach clear, the NVA moved closer toward the perimeter. NVA troops attacked Hill 64 one day following the fall of Lang Vei. It is a small eminence to the northwest of Khe Sanh near the Rock Quarry. 1st Plotoon, Alpha Company; 1/9th Marines had the bunkers.

In the early hours on February 8th, Hill 64 was attacked by a battalion belonging to the 101D Regiment of NVA 325C Division. After a sudden and heavy mortar bombardment by the NVA, they blasted through the wire, using Bangalore torpedoes. Then, they rushed inside. Many Americans were killed by AK47 fire or thrown grenades.

Just 15 minutes later Lieutenant Francis Lovely rallied 22 troops into a much smaller perimeter. 43 more were left severely injured or dead in the wreckage. At dawn, Alpha Company and Delta Company, along with the support of armored vehicles, set out from Rock Quarry. Captain Henry Radcliffe commanded the relief force which violently drove NVA off Hill 64. 150 NVA personnel were killed in the attack on Hill 64 by the NVA. One of them was a map-wielding officer, who showed him how to route tank attacks into Khe Sanh.

At the onset of such attacks, the Americans intensified their Operation Niagara airstrikes. This included everything from bombing with napalm to large-scale bombing by B-52D Arclight mission. The number of ordnance dropped in one day was often greater than the bombing of World War II, which was by a margin as high as 3:1. An NVA soldier from 304 Division vividly recalled how the extraordinary firepower was brought to bear.

Here, the fighting is fiercer than at any other location. It is even more intense here than at Co Roong, Dien Bien Phu. Except for those fighting, we all live underground. We are in the 60th-day and B-52 continue to dump bombs onto our territory. Visitors who come to the area will inform you that it is a place where bombs are poured. All vegetation, animals and even those who live underground or deep in caves, have been destroyed. One can only see red earth (Rottman. 2005, 77).

American bombers and airstrikes are so precise and effective that any location with suspicious activity or indications of NVA force gathering was destroyed. The bombardments continued all day and night with only a few moments between the loud blast of bombs echoing across a quarter. The NVA heavy weapons, large artillery pieces built with enormous labor in the mountains of Laos, dropped several hundred shells every day on Khe Sanh. The 155mm howitzers also contributed to the bombardment. Further in, mortar units also harassed American soldiers.

The Marines at Khe Sanh weren't content to retreat within their walls despite being subjected a bombardment and other difficult living conditions. Despite NVA propaganda being repeated often in American media, Leathernecks remained aggressively determined, despite all the falsehoods.

Their snipers as well as machine gun teams and recoilless firearms searched for smoke, muzzle flashes and other signs to enable them fire back against NVA mortar and sniper teams on the slopes. The Marine mortar squads were constantly engaged in counterbattery firing against NVA mortar positions. Marines stationed at Hill 881S had direct fire on one of the NVA launch sites. They "hosed it off" with M-60 machinegun bullets and rounds of their 106mm reload rifles whenever they saw rockets emerging from it.

A NVA Sniper shot and seriously wounded 10 Marines on Hill 81S in one incident. The enemy responded in typical North Vietnamese fashion by firing mortars upon a Medevac helicopter attempting to land. For some time, the sniper remained elusive, but finally, Marines noticed a flashes of sunlight in his scope high up in an oak tree. India Company's Recoilless Rifle Gunner, 106mm in length, sent a flechette Beehive through the branches. A deadly blast from 5,000 steel flechettes or needles projected at ultrasonic speeds caused by the flechette Beehive. A cloud of wood and torn leaf debris, along with bloody bits from the sniper, flew in all directions.

A second sniper replaced him quickly and was also proving to have good shooting skills. He was killed again by the Marines with the 106mm recoilless weapon, however, his time in the field was short. The NVA sniper number three proved to be quite the opposite.

His replacement [...] wasn't even close to what he was. The misfit spent between 20-30 rounds per daily and struggled for nearly a week with no injuries. [...] When the Marines had brought the 106 to position for the 3rd time [...], one private approached company commander with a proposition. "Skipper," he said, "If we get them, they'll just put him in a position where he can shoot." He hasn't hit anybody so why not just keep him there until they do." The sniper's incompetence saved his own life. He went on blasting away for the rest, and never touched another soul (Shore, 1977,73).

Although it's impossible to prove this, it seems that the third-sniper may have devised a clever method to survive battle. A secret agreement was made with Marines. In this contract, he missed his target and the Marines refused to kill him.

Each Arclight attack was conducted by B-52D planes. They saturated an area of approximately 1 miles long and half a mile wide with hundreds, 750, and 500 lb explosives. B-52Ds dropped more than 76,000 tons worth of bombs in support to Khe Sanh. This doesn't account for fighter-bomber hits, helicopter gunships as well as AC-47 "Spooky", American gunships and American artillery.

NVA successfully shot down a KC-130 Hercules fuel tanker aircraft on February 10, creating a firestorm on the airstrip that killed half a dozen and injuring a further six. Following this, the Americans decided that landing C-130 Hercules Transports was an unreasonable risk. Due to their immense size, these aircraft were difficult to takeoff, landing, and taxi. They became a prime target for rockets and NVA artillery.

Without the C-130 Hercules' vast cargo capability, the base couldn't be sustained. While C-123 Providers were important, they couldn't supply the material required to keep Khe Sanh afloat.

In 1964, the Hercules was designed to skim just a few inches above the runway. The massive cargo hatch was left open. Parachutes deployed on the ground plucking pallets from the interior for landing on the airstrip's surface with parachutes. This technique enabled the Americans to stop C-130s actually landing at Khe Sanh and maintain a full rate in resupply. However, there were still risks. According to one C-130 pilot, he served his country in Vietnam as a C-130 Pilot.

Ground-to-air flame was [...] much heavier and closer towards the aircraft at Khe Sanh's landing approach (Nalty, 1986: 43).

Marine outposts at the hills were supplied by twin-rotor Boeing CH-46 Sea Knights. Although landing at Khe Sanh is a more risky operation than landing on the hills, these operations quickly left the hillslopes with many wrecked helicopters. Marines responded by creating "Super Gaggle." This was a group composed of CH-46s and medical helicopters. It was accompanied with helicopter gunships as well as a Douglas A-4 Skyhawk Skyhawk subsonic strike aircraft. The A-4 Skyhawks dispersed known or suspected NVA Antiaircraft Units with tear gas bombs, rockets, cannonfire and cannon fire, along with setting up smokescreens to protect helicopter landings. The Super Gaggle provided protection and helicopter losses decreased precipitously from mid to late February.

Under night, small NVA units kept an eye on the Khe Sanh defenses. These led innumerable brief firefights involving Marine defenders against North Vietnamese scouting team during the last part of the 77 day siege.

NVA decided to take to the air as they had no air power. NVA, utilizing their territory gained through the seizing of Khe Sanh village & Lang Vei, started at Hill 461, south of Khe Sanh. From there, the NVA extended a network, fortified from bunker strongpoints., to the base's southern wire. This work was done in February. The Americans bombed the trenches but were unable stop them from creeping within 25 meters of the wire.

The NVA appeared to have made a serious attempt at overrunning the base in the late hours of the morning of March 1, 1968. The NVA used its trench lines to move at minimum a full battalion (304 Division) into position to attack 37th ARVN Ranger

Battalion. However, South Vietnamese and Americans saw them and prepared a fatal welcome.

Before the NVA could ever leave their trenches artillery brought them under severe fire. Captain Harry Baig, 26th Marines, Target Information Officer, described the process:

The fires took this form: A three-sided wooden box, with one side open, was placed at the presumed or actual location of an assault unit. This mission was carried out by three battery. A fourth battery then sealed the remainder of the box's open side and moved forward into the box as a piston within its cylindrical. Once it had reached the far side of box, it began to roll back. The box contained an enemy force that could not escape. They could not escape the rolling barrage and its piston effect. Hammel, 1989. 325.

The bombardment proved even more deadly for Marine artillery which used COFRAM-cluster munitions. The majority of the battalion was trapped in this deadly "box," and did not even leave their jumping-off areas. ARVN Rangers located 75 bodies the following day, all smashed and torn up by the rolling bombardment.

Sensors and reconnaissance planes indicated that two other battalions in the 304 Division were moving up to help the anticipated breakthrough of a leading battalion. Two huge Arc Light raids were conducted by B-52Ds on each battalion to disintegrate the supporting forces. Shortly thereafter Bru Montagnards retorted that there were approximately 500 NVA bodies left by their comrades at the tracks southwest of the base.

Khe Sanh was not directly affected, although the NVA did lose a battalion and possibly more of the 304 Division. The attack was clearly designed to make a decisive push to enter the base's defenses, and to eventually insert the entire NVA Division there. It was a disastrous failure for the North Vietnamese. It was also a fire mission that proved to be heavy and anticlimactic for the defenders.

An interesting aspect of the assault was the reason why the NVA chose not to use their armour. South Vietnamese claimed that they heard the tanks move but did not find any on their subsequent sweeps. Despite having more PT-76 guns than those taken out at Lang Vei by the NVA, they disappeared mysteriously from battleground.

March 1st marked the end of the NVA's assault on Khe Sanh. Instead, they attacked the base and continued firing. NVA troops ambushed American troop patrols. The enemy then made desultory attempts to "turn around" the ARVN by spreading propaganda. However, NVA documents captured from this period show large North

Vietnamese desertions, which in some cases reduced fighting strength by half.

The North Vietnamese also increased their propaganda during this period, claiming that they never intended the base to be taken and that the obliterated battalion, or division, was a mere diversion. These pretenses were destroyed by Captain Moyers Shore.

Communists also tried selling the line that 20,000 North Vietnamese had 'tied down' the 26th Marines. This argument was full of bitter grapes. This kind of logic is similar in that a defeated coach would say that he didn't really want win the game but only kept the other team "tied up" for an hr (Shore 1997, 77).

The NVA paid dearly for not staying in Khe Sanh, where they were attacked on March 1. After the cloudy, foggy, and rainy January and February, March brought sunshine and beautiful weather. American aircraft circled the skies striking at the smallest sign of movement. Despite avoiding direct attacks against Khe Sanh and revealing their movements in clear visibility, many NVA unit suffered substantial losses from American airstrikes.

Operation Pegasus was an American military plan to "relieve" or reinforce Khe Sanh. High command organized a Provisional Corps, which included the 101st Airborne Division as well the 1st Cavalry Division, 3rd Marine Division (3rd Marines), ARVN units, and several others. The Americans would've sent the force sooner but mop up operations around Hue after the Tet Offensive delayed it.

Ca Lu was built by the Americans to support their operation. The base included an airstrip as well as a defensive base. It could handle C-123 and C-7 Caribou vehicles. LZ (Landing Zone Stud was the base's nickname.

Marines from Khe Sanh launched the attack on Hill 471 in a local operation to stop NVA operations at the south perimeter. Although the Americans were able to kill 123 NVAs, forcing the rest to temporarily retreat from the area, they also suffered 9 KIA, more than 100 WIA, a costly exercise that didn't gain them any ground.

April 1st saw LZ Stud's 3rd Marines move towards Khe Sanh. There were two battalions leading this charge. Initially, the 1st Cavalry was held back by bad weather. However, their meteorological conditions improved and they started leapfrogging ahead to the 3rd Marines when they moved westward towards the base.

Marines encountered very weak NVA resistance as they moved through thick jungles and mountain terrain. They found several abandoned NVA camp, including one with running water and furniture. This allowed them to enjoy small verandas right in front the bunkers. The NVA captured large amounts of food from these camps. However, they only found a few weapons and ammunition.

Operation Pegasus saw only two notable actions. The NVA held Old French Fort in its hands against the advancing relief force and had it removed. The NVA counterattack mounted a counterattack to retake Hill 471, the second occurring during the seizure.

Three companies of Marines from the 1st Battalion moved out of Rock Quarry on April 4th at 6AM to attack Hill 471. The assault was preceded with heavy American bombardment. NVA observators called in artillery support in Laos from the Laos battery during the advance. The huge shells, which were trying to send red clay fountains and shattered trees into the skyward, could not find the proper range to strike Marines.

As the Marines made their way up the hill, the NVA came to their aid with automatic weapons fire and showers of grenades. As his award citation explains, Corporal Barry Thoryk earned the Navy Cross by personally dismantling several machine guns positions.

Corporal Thoryk was injured in multiple fragmentation wounds and had to refuse medical treatment. Instead, he launched an aggressive attack against an enemy machine guns position, killing three of its guards. After exhausting his ammunition, Corporal Thoryk quickly obtained an opponent weapon and fired [...]. He continued to maneuver forward, grabbing hand grenades of enemy soldiers and throwing them at hostile positions as his progress (Hammel, 1989, 422-421).

The Marines cleared out the hill in about 30 minutes. They discovered 30 NVA on top of the mountain and captured many young, scared soldiers. The 66th Regiment 304 Division - already attacked in the unsuccessful March 1st attacks on Khe Sanh – attacked Khe Sanh hill immediately after an artillery bombing. They proved to be easy targets for the Marines who were illuminated with starshells. Marines killed 122 NVA troops and left 19 wounded. The NVA fled in the darkness.

As a gesture of support to the South Vietnamese people, the relief force flown a company belonging to the 3rd ARVN Task Force in Khe Sanh on the 6th of April, before American units arrived. So, the ARVN troops became officially the first reliever troops to arrive in Khe Sanh.

Khe Sanh was defended by American troops belonging to the 7th Cavalry Squadron. They were contacted on April 8th. Operation Pegasus officially continued up to April 14th. The three divisions arrived on the scene and reestablished contact between Khe Sanh, American forces elsewhere in South Vietnam. Since the Marines didn't feel at risk of being overrun, they did not celebrate the men joining forces. Instead, they simply saw Operation Pegasus, which was the prelude to taking up the fight against the enemy, as a celebration.

Operation Scotland II succeeded. In it, the united American forces hunted NVA army unit in the area and destroyed their weapons. Operation Charlie began on June 19th and saw the Americans demolish Khe Sanh, abandoning it due to political factors.

The Americans lost 274 men and 2,541 were wounded during the battle for Khe Sanh. The ARVN, on the other hand, suffered 229 KIA and 436 WIA. The Americans claimed that 10,000 NVA soldiers had died, while a secret MACV intelligence analysis put the figure at 5,550. The NVA claimed 2 469 combat deaths and 1 436 injuries. Operation Scotland II also cost the Americans 485 deaths. The Americans received 3,304 confirmed NVA deaths in action in exchange for Operation Scotland II. One soldier of the American Special Forces made a grim joke about it:

Khe Sanh is the most heavily blasted area on Earth. It's so difficult to do a body count even with microscopes (Ankony, 2006, 157).

The NVA found the Battle of Khe Sanh to be an expensive adventure. While all indications point to the seriousness of their attempt to seize this base, they lacked military experience and the right equipment. David Lownds was the commander of 26th Marines stationed at Khe Sanh and provided perhaps the most comprehensive summary of Leathernecks' situation.

I've been with Khe Sanh for nine-months, and if they keep them supplied, I could be here for another nine months (Shore, 1977, 84).

Khe Sanh could almost be described as an American victory. The US Marines successfully captured Khe Sanh. The North Vietnamese surrendered and left the battlefield in American hands. Despite the amount of artillery they had and the fact that they used tanks in one of the assaults, the Vietnamese forces were also more severely wounded than their enemies.

General Westmoreland was proud of the American success. He wanted to make the American victory a springboard for a major Laos offensive. This was prevented due to political factors and not military factors.

Uncertainty remains about the motivations of North Vietnamese leaders for launching Khe Sanh's siege. Despite relations between Vietnam (USA) and Vietnam becoming more normalized during the first quarter of this century, the Vietnamese are not forthcoming about their views regarding the war. The official narrative of the war is still sparse, veiled, or completely silent in many instances.

The facts support multiple scenarios. One possibility is the NVA's desire to win one crushing defeat over the Americans. This would have demoralized them and caused them to retreat to an American Dien Bien Phu. In this case, the Vietnamese were defeated spectacularly and suffered only a bloody loss.

Another possibility would be that the North Vietnamese intended for the attack to distract from American forces just before the Tet Offensive. They had partial success, if that was the intention. Khe Sanh did indeed take up large amounts American resources for several weeks. The Tet Offensive evolved into a military victory for the Americans. Initial successes soon collapsed when the Americans destroyed the Viet Cong.

Khe Sanh would be considered a North Vietnamese victory even if the purpose was pure political. Khe Sanh was effectively a propaganda victory by the North due to the American press being hostile to the US army and siding with them. The NVA carried out the action. American citizens were presented with a negative and hostile viewpoint by the media.

Khe Sanh became yet another piece of ammunition as part of a concentrated effort by the media in order to shift American public opinion against war. The media also created protests and other political turmoil. America yielded the fight to communists thanks to the mobilization by news services of public opposition - despite fact that the Tet Offensive (and the subsequent Cambodian Campaign) were military successes that could have led directly to the North's defeat if pursued.

Chapter 6: The Vietnam War Summarized

Vietnam War, also known by the 2nd Indochina War or the 1st November 1955, was fought in Vietnam, Laos and Cambodia. It was the second Indochina Wars. China, South Korea (and other communist allies), backed North Vietnam. While the United States and South Korea, Australia (and other anti-communist friendly countries), backed South Vietnam.

Some believe it was a Cold War-era proxy battle. U.S. participation ended in 1973.

The First Indochina War began the conflict. This war pitted the French colonial administration against Viet Minh's left-wing innovative force. Following the 1954 French withdrawal from Indochina the U.S.A. provided military and monetary support for the South Vietnamese federal administration.

The Viet Cng or VC, also known under the Front country de liberation du Sud Viet

Nam/NLF (National Freedom Front), is a South Vietnamese typical Front that began a guerrilla program in the South. It was led by North Vietnam. North Vietnam, in support of insurgents attacked Laos around the mid-1950s. They built the Ho Chi Minh Path, which was designed to enhance and provide for the Viet Cng. Under President John F. Kennedy's MAAG program the U.S. increased its engagement by roughly 1,000 army consultants between 1959 and 1964. This was in addition to the 23,000-plus U.S. soldiers who were deployed in that year. 1963 saw the North Vietnamese send 40,000 soldiers to South Vietnam in order to fight.

A United States destroyer was reported by North Vietnamese to have hit a swift attack boat in the Gulf of Tonkin on August 1, 1964.

In reaction, President Lyndon B. Johnson signed the Gulf of Tonkin Resolution. He was granted broad authority to increase

American military involvement in Vietnam. Johnson ordered for the first times the release and augmentation of force levels to 184,000.

People's Army of Vietnam or NVA, was also allied with the USA and South Vietnamese troops. Despite the lack of success, the U.S.A. had a large army accumulation. Robert McNamara the U.S. secretary of defense, was one the war's main designers and was making appointments for success. United States and South Vietnamese troops used air supremacy as well as frustrating firepower to carry out searches and damage operations using ground forces and weapons. The United States launched a large-scale tactical battle project to target North Vietnam as well as Laos. North Vietnam was backed by China as well as the Soviet Union.

Domestic support started to decrease as the VC or PAVN began massive offensives in 1968, the Tet Offensive. After a period of overlook following Tet the Army of the Republic of Vietnam's (ARVN), was enlarged and imitated U.S.A. Dogma. The VC suffered tremendous losses throughout the Tet Offensive. :

The CIA operated the Phoenix Program, which significantly reduced the VC's abilities and subscription. The VC rebels possessed almost no land in South Vietnam at year's end. In 1969, their enrollment was down by more 80 percent. This reflected a decline in guerrilla operations and called for the increased use north of PAVN routine fighters. North Vietnam formed a Provisional Revolutionary Federal Government to South Vietnam in 1969. This was in order to increase the visibility of the weakened VC. But the South Vietnamese guerrillas were marginalized and the PAVN started more traditional mixed arms operations. By 1970, the northerners accounted more than 70% for communist soldiers in south Vietnam, and the southern-dominated VC programs had disappeared. North Vietnam used Laos as its first supply route. Cambodia was used by Vietnam too in 1967. The United States started bombarding Cambodian-bound Laos in 1969. The Cambodian National Assembly dragged Norodom Sihanouk to the ground. This resulted in a PAVN invasion, which was requested by the Khmer Rouge. This escalated the Cambodian Civil War.

Following the election of Richard Nixon as President of the United States in 1969, a program known as "Vietnamization" was launched. This included an increase of ARVN and USA forces being marginalized and discouraged by domestic resistance. By 1972, most of the United States' ground fighters had left. There was no more support from the United States for weapons and other support. The U.S.A. assisted ARVN stopped the first and largest motorized PAVN military offensive during the Easter Assault. The attack resulted to heavy casualties on both the sides and South Vietnam's inability to dominate the PAVN. However the ARVN wasn't able to retake all the terrain it had, leaving the army in precarious condition. All USA forces were withdrawn under the Paris Peace Accords which took effect in January 1973. The Case - Church Change, which was enacted in 1973 by the U.S. Congress, effectively ended U.S. direct army participation.

The Peace Accords was quickly breached and fighting continued for 2 additional years. The Khmer Rouge took over Phnom Penh April 17, 1975. In 1975, the PAVN assumed control of Saigon April 30th. 1975 was the year 1975. This marked a halt to the war. North Vietnam and South Vietnam were reunited that year.

The struggle was enormous. The ARVN, which had nearly one-million men in its ranks, was the 4th largest military force in the world. It was established by 1970. The Vietnamese people suffered significant losses as a result of the dispute. According to estimates, the number killed and the number of those who died in combat ranged from 966,000 - three million. 275,000-- 310,000 Cambodians; 20,000-- 62,000 Laotians; 58,220 USA soldiers were killed during the fighting. There are 1,626 missing.

Following the Vietnam War's lull, there was a reemergence of the Sino-Soviet divide. The dispute between North Vietnam with its Cambodian advocates in Royal Federal Government of National Union of Kampuchea was rekindled almost instantly by a series of Khmer Rouge border raids. This led to the Cambodian—-Vietnam War. Chinese soldiers invaded Vietnam during the Sino-Vietnamese War. These actions triggered border wars that lasted up to 1991. The unified Vietnam launched revolutions in all 3 countries. The Vietnamese boat people, along with the greater Indochina refugee issue, were helped by the end and beginning of the Third Indochina War. Many refugees fled Indochina (primarily, southern Vietnam), where an estimated 250,000 drowned at sea. This dispute led to what was called the "Vietnam Syndrome" by the United States. It was a public hostility toward American army interference in foreign governments. This, together with the Watergate scandal, contributed to the country's trust issues in the 1970s.

Chapter 7: What Caused the War?

The U.S.A. Army, the Army of the Republic of Vietnam and the U.S. Army were opposed to People's Army of Vietnam. Also known as the North Vietnamese Army, NVA, or NVA in English, and the National Front for the Freedom of South Vietnam (NLF), also known under the name Viet Cong (VC in English).

Indochina belonged to France from the end of the 19th century through the middle 20th century. The Viet Minh a Communist-led, typical front led Ho Chi Minh, fought the Japanese in the Second World War. It was supported by China, the Soviet Union and the United States. They received Japanese weapons after Japan surrendered. Ho Chi Minh (DRV), announced the Democratic Republic of Vietnam, V-J Day (September 2nd). The DRV ruled Vietnam for twenty-days as the only civil government after Emperor Boi (who had ruled under Japanese supervision) resigned. French forces seized the regional DRVfederal government, which was established in 1945 on September 23rd. French forces gradually retook Indochina. After failing in reaching an agreement, Viet Minh launched rebellion against French control. The First Indochina War resulted from the escalation hostilities which began in December 1946.

The Cold War had made the conflict more linked to it by the 1950s. China and Soviet Union accepted the Viet Minh's Democratic Republic of Vietnam, which was based in Hanoi as the lawful government of Vietnam in the January 1950. The U.S.A. acknowledged the French-backed Government of Vietnam in Saigon that was ordered by the deposed Emperor Boi as Vietnam's authentic federal government. Washington policymakers were convinced that the Korean War erupted in June 1950 because of Soviet-directed communist expansionism.

Chinese army consultants became involved in the support of the Viet Minh beginning July 1950. PRC weapons were used to transform the Viet Minh's guerilla forces into routine soldiers. The Armed force Help and Advisory Group of the USA (MAAG) was established in September 1950 by the US to analyse French help requests, advise on technique and train Vietnamese forces.

In 1954, $1 billion had been spent by the USA to support the French Army effort. This was eighty percent.

The Battle of Dien-Bien Phu occurred in 1954. United States ships cruised to the Gulf of Tonkin for security flights. France and the United States were also discussing the possibility of applying 3 tactical nuclear arms. However, conflicting reports about how serious and by whom this was discussed are not accurate and contradictory. Richard Nixon was then the Vice President. He stated that the Joint Chiefs of Staff created preparations to support France with small tactical nuclear arms. Nixon, who was often referred to by as a "hawk", expressed concern about Vietnam and said that the USA may need "put American lads inside."

Dwight D. Eisenhower, President, made participation to the war conditional for British support. But the British resisted it. Eisenhower was afraid of the U.S. becoming involved in a land issue in Asia. He chose to not intervene militarily.

American intelligence estimates didn't believe France had a chance of winning the war.

The French soldiers of Dien Bien Phu fell on May 7, 1954. The French army presence was cut off in Indochina after the defeat. The Geneva Conference witnessed the French reach a ceasefire deal with Viet Minh. Cambodian, Laos, Vietnam, and Laos were granted independence.

Vietnam was temporarily divided at 17th parallel, at the time of 1954 Geneva peace talks. Ho Chi Minh had hoped to extend the fighting in the South, but his Chinese friends encouraged that he could take power through electoral means. Under the Geneva Accords civilians were able move easily between these two interim states for three hundred days. In 1956, nationwide elections were held in order to form a single federal government. Around one million northerners, mostly Catholic minorities emigrated south to escape Communist persecution. This was in reaction to an American psychological warfare effort (Edward Lansdale, Central Intelligence Agency) that increased anti Catholic belief amongst Vietnamese. The CIA incorrectly believed the U.S. planned to unleash atomic bombs upon Hanoi. A $93 million US-sponsored effort was used to manage the exodus. It included the use the Seventh Fleet as a means of transferring refugees. The Ngo Nh Dim administration received significant anti-communist support by the mostly Catholic refugees from northern Vietnam. Dim mostly occupied key positions in the federal government, mainly with Catholics from north and center.

Around 130,000 Revolutionary Regroupees made the trip to North America to seek "regroupment," in an effort to go back to South Africa within two years. In the south, Viet Minh left 5,000-ten thousand cadres as a foundation for future resistance. In April 1956, South Vietnam saw the end of French forces. At the exact moment, People's Republic of China pulled out from North Vietnam.

There were many agrarian reforms that the North Vietnamese federal Government implemented between 1953-1956. These included "lease decrease", and "land réforme." This led directly to political injustice. North Vietnamese witnesses stated that one execution was done for every 160 people in each hamlet at the time. This resulted in a preliminary number of 100,000 executions. Scientists accepted at the time a lower estimate of 50,000 executions since the Red River Delta was the focus of this project. On the other hand, files declassified from Hungarian or Vietnamese archives reveal that the actual executions were much lower than was originally reported. However they are still over 13,500. Hanoi's leaders admitted that they had "excesses" when executing the plan in 1956. Most of the property was returned to their original owners.

In the meantime the south created the State of Vietnam. Ngo nh Dim was the Prime Minister and Emperor Boi. At the 1954 Geneva Conference the U.S. federal Government and Ngo nh Dim of the State of Vietnam did not sign anything. The Vietnamese non-communist delegation was vehemently opposed to any division of Vietnam. However the French accepted Phm Van ng's proposal to reunify Vietnam through elections managed under "regional commissions". The US came up with the "American Plan," which was later referred to as the United Kingdom and South Vietnam. The Soviet delegation turned it down because it required that marriage elections were held under UN guidance. "With regard to the comment made in Vietnam by the agent of State of Vietnam," USA added, "The U.S.A. has not changed its standard view that tribes are sovereign and have the right of making their own decisions about their future."

The domino Hypothesis was promoted by Eisenhower, who believed that if one country became communist, it would cause communism to spread to all neighboring countries. John F. Kennedy, a United States senator at the time, stated that Burma was among those countries whose security might be endangered if the Red Tide of Communism reached Vietnam.

Chapter 8: Kennedy's Participation

In the 1960 USA election for the governmental office, Senator John F. Kennedy defeated Richard M. Nixon. Kennedy says that Eisenhower was correct to warn about Vietnam and Laos. However, Latin America and Europe "loomed more than Asia in his opinions."

Kennedy approved the Bay of Pigs attack in April 1961. The Soviet Premier Nikita Shrushchev was the first person he encountered when they met in Vienna during June 1961. Just sixteen months later the Cuban Rocket Crisis (16-18 October 1962) was transmitted live over the internet. As the Cold War drew closer to nuclear war, the USA increased the preparedness of Strategic Air Command (SAC), assets to DEFCON2.

The Cold War Foreign Technique was the one that Kennedy followed. Kennedy faced 4 crises in 1961. There were 50,000 Americans in South Korea. Kennedy also dealt with the failure of Bay of Pigs Intrusion (which he had authorized in April), settlement negotiations between Pathet Lao communist movements in May (" Kennedy avoided Laos' rugged terrain, which was no battlefield for American troops") and the Bay of Pigs Intrusion (which he had authorised in April). In August, the Berlin Wall was constructed, and the Cuban Rocket Crisis took place in October. Kennedy believed that a failure to take control of communist growth would permanently damage the USA's credibility. Kennedy was determined not to allow communists in Vietnam to succeed by "drawing the boundary in the sand." "Now we need to make our strength reputable," he said to James Reston, The New York Times, shortly after his Vienna top meeting.

Kennedy believed Dim and his soldiers would have to fight against the insurgents in South Vietnam by their own means in his approach to South Vietnam. He opposed the installation of American battle soldiers. He said that "introducing significant U.S. forces there now, while it might provide an at-first beneficial army effect," would in fact have negative and unfavorable army ramifications. In contrast, the South Vietnamese military was of poor quality. The ARVN's demise was caused by poor management, corruption, as well as political promotions. As the rebellion gained traction, there were more guerrilla assaults. While Hanoi did support the VietCong, this was not the only problem.

Kennedy stressed the importance of determining if Soviet space and rocket capabilities had outstripped America's. Kennedy was open to using special forces for counterinsurgency warfare in a developing country under threat by communist rebels. Kennedy believed that Green Berets' combative techniques could be used after a Soviet incursion in Europe.

Failed actions, such as the Battle of p Bc of January 2, 1963, where a small Viet Cong band won a struggle against a South Vietnamese force that was larger and better equipped, were a hallmark of the ARVN's failure to be efficient.

Five U.S. war helicopters carrying ARVN soldiers to the Vietcong were also killed, leaving only 18 Vietcong fighters. Hunh Van Cao, the IV Corps leader, was Dim's most trusted general. Cao, a Catholic who had rose on faith rather than capability and his important role in the defense of coup attempts was to keep his men unified. He had also been thrown up during a communist invasion. Some Washington strategists thought Dim was incapable or unwilling to beat the communists. After the failed coup attempts in 1960 and 1962, Dim seemed more interested in stopping them and was paranoid. He partially blamed USA support for his paranoia. Robert F. Kennedy claims that Dim was determined not to accept concessions. He was a hard man to convince ..." [117.

Following the Hu Pht.n murders, 9 unarmed Buddhists opposed to the restriction on the Buddhist flag being displayed on Vesak the Buddha's day, discontent with Dims's policies emerged in May 1963. The Hu Pht n murders of 9 unarmed Buddhists in May 1963 prompted a flood of criticisms about inequitable policies that favor the Catholic and its followers over those from the Buddhist majority. Ngo Nh Thc Thc, Dim's older sibling, was Archbishop for Hu and powerfully blurred boundaries between church and state. Thuc held his anniversary events shortly before Vesak's federal government was supportive. Also, often, Vatican flags were shown. There were also stories that Catholic paramilitaries destroyed Buddhist pagodas at the time Dim was in power. Dim refused the Buddhist bulk's needs and took responsibility for the casualties. Colonel Le Quang Tung's ARVN

Special Forces dedicated to Dim's younger brother Ngo Thien Nhu attacked Pagodas around Vietnam in August 1963. It caused extensive damage and loss of life.

U.S.A. authorities first began to look into the possibility for routine changes around the middle of 1963. The State Department attempted to make a coup, but Dim was wanted by the Defense Department. Dim's younger brother Nhu who supervised secret authorities and unique troops and was generally viewed as the mastermind Buddhist repression and, in a wider sense, the architect of Ngo family authority was one of the reforms. This proposal was sent with cable television number 243 to the USA Embassy in Saigon.

The CIA called generals who were lining up to remove Dim. It assured them that neither the U.S.A. would oppose their actions nor penalize them by cutting off supply. President Dim was arrested and executed with his brother, on November 2, 1963. Maxwell Taylor remembers that Kennedy was not informed and he "hurried to leave the room with an expression of shock, discouragement and anger on his face."

Kennedy had not anticipated Dim's assassination. Henry Cabot Lodge the U.S.A. ambassador, South Vietnam, welcomed the leaders of the coup to the embassy, and applauded. Kennedy was told that the possibilities for a shorter dispute now exist. Kennedy wrote Lodge praises for his "great job"

As a result, Mayhem was created. Hanoi profited by the circumstances and increased support for the insurgents. South Vietnam suffered a period in which one army's federal government was toppled after another. The communists considered each successive ruler to be a puppet of the Americans. However, Dim's faults aside, Robert McNamara asserted that his qualifications as an nationalist were unmatched.

U.S.A. military advisers were stationed at every level in the South Vietnamese military. The Americans were chastised however for not taking into account the political nature. The Kennedy administration was determined to refocus USA efforts towards pacification. In this context, it was meant to combat the rising danger of rebellion and "won" the hearts of the citizens. Washington army management opposed any U.S.A. Consultants participation. General Paul Harkins who was the leader for U.S. forces South Vietnam expected victory by Christmas 1963.

The CIA however was downhearted warning that the Viet Cong had "the most part" retained de facto control over the country and were gradually increasing their overall strength.

Paramilitary officials from the CIA's Unique Activities Division gave instruction and orders to Hmong people in Vietnam and Laos. These native forces, which numbered in excess of 10,000, were deployed to direct action against North Vietnamese supporters and Communist Pathet-Lao warriors. The Phoenix Program was also managed and supervised by the CIA.

Chapter 9: Johnson's Involvement

President John F. Kennedy's death occurred on November 20, 1963. Lyndon B. Johnson's vice president had not been involved with Vietnam policy since before he became president. Johnson, however, quickly focused on this dispute once he was elected. On November twenty-fourth 1963, Johnson said that "The war on communism... should to be signed up... with... power and devotion." Johnson was aware of South Vietnam's rapidly changing circumstances, but he continued to follow the common domino principle validation for protecting South Vietnam: retreat or surrender would jeopardize other nations beyond the war. Some people claim that North Vietnam did not seek to undermine other non communist routines in Southeast Asia.

The army's innovative council was composed of twelve members. General Dng Van Minh was later described as "a design in sleepiness" by Stanley Karnow (a reporter on the scene), who ordered this council.

"Will this man be strong enough to handle the challenges?" Lodge, frustrated toward the end the year, called home about Minh. General Nguyn Khanh defeated Minh's routine in January 1964.

There was constant instability within the army. There were several coups over a short time. Not all of which succeeded.

The Tonkin Gulf Event

While conducting intelligence operations off the coast of North Vietnam in August 1964, the USS Maddox allegedly fired on and injured 6 torpedo-boats that were being followed it in the Gulf of Tonkin. 2 days later, Maddox was the target of another attack by the USS Turner Delight in the exact area. The details of the attacks were not clear. Lyndon Johnson, Undersecretary for State George Ball, stated that sailors out were possible to have been facing flying fish.

According to an undated NSA report, which was published in 2005 it states that there was no attack on August 4.

After the 2nd attack, vindictive battles were fought. Congress passed the Gulf of Tonkin Resolution (August 7, 1964).

[The resolution gave Johnson the right "to take all necessary means for pushing back any armistice against the US armed forces and to stop the ensuing hostilities," which Johnson considered as allowing him to intensify his war. Johnson mentioned that he wouldn't "commit American boys" to fighting in a war which, according to me, should be fought solely by the Asian lads to protect their country.

The National Security Council encouraged the intensification of the North Vietnam war in three phases. Operation Flaming Dart, which was led by Soviet Premier Alexei

Kosygin, was launched to respond to an attack against a United States Army centre in Pleiku on February 7th 1965. Operation Rolling Thunder was expanded to include ground support activities as well the plane barrage. The battle project, which lasted for 3 years, threatened to degrade North Vietnamese air defenses. It was also intended increase South Vietnamese spirit. Rolling Thunder attacked the north with a thousand tons of rockets/bombs and rockets between November 1968 and March 1965.

The Lao Bombardments

Bombs were dropped on North Vietnam but not all. Operation Snap Roll for example was an attack on some parts of VietCong roads and the PAVN road network. There were many. The supply path for Ho Chi Minh, which passed through Laos or Cambodia, was one of them. The neutral Laos had become a civil war between a US-backed Laotian federal administration and the

Pathet Lao with its North Vietnamese advocates.

The U.S. launched large-scale air strikes against Pathet Lao (and PAVN) forces in order to stop the collapsed Royal main federal Government and the Ho Chi Minh Path. The U.S.A. exploded 2 million bombs upon Laos between 1964-1973. This almost equals to the 2.1million bombs dropped on Europe during The Second World War. Laos is the largest regularly bombarded state in history according to its population.

The goal to end North Vietnam and the VietCong was never achieved. Still, U.S. Curtis LeMay was the Chief of Staff for the Flying Force. He had long advocated saturation war in Vietnam. LeMay wrote about the communists that "we're gonna bomb them back to the Stone Age."

Ground War in the United States

3,500 U.S.A. Army Militaries arrived in South Vietnam near Da Nang on March 8th, 1965.

This was also the start of America's ground project. The United States received little to no public support for the release. Da Nang Air Base was the Militaries' first objective. The initial deployment of 3,500 troops in March 1965 led to an increase of approximately 200,000 soldiers by December 1965.

For a long period, the USA armed Force has been well trained in aggressive war. No matter how political their intentions may be, American leaders are institutionally and emotionally not prepared to defend a target.

General William Westmoreland warned Admiral U. S. Grant Sharp Jr. (leader of United States Pacific forces) that the matter was urgent. He added, "I am confident that with their excitement movement and firepower, United States Soldiers can effectively take the War to the NLF [Viet Cong]". With this suggestion Westmoreland was encouraging a radical change in

America's defensive posture. The U.S.A. dedication ended in open-ended, with the abandonment of ARVN.

Westmoreland was predicting victory by the end in 1967.

Johnson, on other hand, did nothing to notify the media about this shift in techniques. Johnson, however, did not notify the media about the change in techniques. He instead stressed the importance for consistency. The U.S. policy shift was dependent on a fight between the VietCong and North Vietnam. The enemies found themselves in a vicious circle, with no way out.

It was rejected that South Vietnam's Federal Government could manage its own affairs.

McNamara and Westmoreland praised the body count strategy in identifying success. It would, therefore, be incorrect.

The PAVN lured American fighters into the hinterlands, at k To and Marine Khe Sanh. These bases were located in Qung Tr Province in the late 1967. Here the USA engaged in a series of skirmishes that they called "The Hill Fights." These attacks became part the red herring that was intended to draw US forces into Central Highlands. Van Tin Dng, also known by the Tet Offensive or the General Offensive, meant that forces could make "direct striking against the American switchboard"-- Saigon Hu Danang, Danang, all the major cities, towns, and key bases . Le Duan was trying to calm the critics of this extended standoff.

He believed this could be achieved through a widespread rebellion in cities, as well as large defections from ARVN during a holiday that lasted throughout the truce.

Over 85,000 VC/PAVN savages assaulted more than one hundred cities during the Tet Offensive.

U.S., South Vietnamese forces were initially surprised at the magnitude, ferocity, planning and execution of the attack on the city. Intrusion of workers and weapons into these cities was discreetly carried out; this attack was an intelligence failure equal to Pearl Harbor.

Most cities were saved within weeks. Hu was the exception. Hu was the historical royal capital. PAVN/Viet Cong troops controlled the majority, castle, and head office in the city. They defended the area for 26 days.

They killed nearly 2,800 Hu locals unarmed and immigrants they believed to be nemesis representative at the time.

American fighters used immense firepower to demolish 80% of the city following the Battle of Hu.

The ARVN Airborne Division (the first Division) and a routine for the USA first Cavalry Division had successfully held off an attack aimed at taking Qung Tr City further north.

Viet Cong/PAVN militants from Saigon took control of areas around the city and targeted critical structures and the Cholon population before being driven out by United States and ARVN forces.

Peter Arnett noted that an infantry leader stated, "It was vital to destroy this hamlet to protect it," during Battle of Bn Tre. (which was eventually overthrown by U.S.A. attack).

Prior to Tet in November 1967 Westmoreland headed a public relation project for President Lyndon B. Johnson. It was designed to support well-known subsidies.

In a speech before the National Press Club, He stated that the war had entered a stage where "the conclusion emerges."

This resulted in Westmoreland's forecasts being thwarted by the Tet Offensive. His overall efficiency has seen a decline in public approval from 48%-36% while his support for war has fallen from 40%-26%.

Johnson was demolished by the American public, media and army as 3 offensives repelled claims of success made in Johnson's administration and army.

Westmoreland was considering using nuclear weapons on Vietnam in a contingency program codenamed Fracture Jaw during 1968. However, the White Home discovered about it and it was put on hold.

Westmoreland's request to have 200,000 more soldiers made was leaked to the general public. Intelligence failures combined with the consequences led him to be fired from command in March 1968. Creighton Absrams was his replacement.

Peace talks between North Vietnam & the USA started in Paris in May 1968.

Settlements remained stagnant for five months, before Johnson granted orders to halt the fighting in North Vietnam. Hanoi knew that it would never be able attain "complete accomplishment" so it adopted a method called "talking, fighting, fighting without talking" where army offensives and settlements were simultaneously conducted.

Johnson decided to withdraw his bid for re-election after pointing out a drop on his approval score from 48% à 36%.

Chapter 10: The Downfall and War Crimes

A wide range of war criminal offenses occurred during the Vietnam War. Both sides committed war criminal offences during the battle. This includes rape. Civilian massacres. Barrage of civilian targets. Terrorism. Extensive use of abuse and the murder of detainees. Theft and arson were also common criminal offenses.

Vietnam War Crimes Working Group (VWCWG), a Pentagon job team, was established in 1968 to examine war criminal activities of United States armed soldiers in Vietnam in the period of the Vietnam War.

A sworn statement from witnesses and status report revealed that 320 of war criminal offenses committed to army authorities had an exact basis.

7 massacres between 1967-1971 left at least 137 dead; 78 additional non-combatants were attacked and killed in attacks that claimed 57 lives, 56 injuries, and 15 sexual

assaults; and 141 cases in the United States of America of U.S.A. troops abusing civilian prisoners or prisoners of war using fists sticks bats water or electric shock. Journalism has exposed many war criminal offenses that remain unsolved, including all the army divisions that served in Vietnam. Rummel estimates that American forces killed roughly 5,500 people between 1960-72. The death toll could range from 4,000 to tens of thousands.

USA forces have created free-fire zones in order to deter Viet Cong fighters and prevent them from safeguarding South Vietnamese communities.

Lewis M. Simons claims that this strategy which included the assumption that anyone entering designated zones is an opponent contender who can be easily targeted with weapons was a grave offense under the laws. Nick Turse wrote in 2013 Kill Anything That Moves. He claimed that the relentless pursuit of higher body count, frequent use of freefire zones and guidelines of engagement, which categorised people escaping fighters or helicopters from Viet Cong as Viet Cong, along with widespread contempt for Vietnamese civilians led to huge civilian casualties. Also, there were numerous war criminal offenses committed primarily by U.S. soldiers.

Turse mentions Objective Rapid Express, a 9th Infantry Division operation John Paul Vann refers to as "some M Lasis."

According to Newsweek publication, at least 5,000 people were killed in the six-month long operation. Around 748 arms were taken, and the main United States army count was 10,889 adversary rivals.

R.J. Rummel estimated that 39,000 people were killed during South Vietnam's Democide Period. Rummel used a series 16,000 to 167,000 to estimate this. Rummel however believed that between 1964 and 1975, 50,000 people had been killed by

South Vietnam. Rummel used a range of 42,000 to 128,000 individuals to determine Rummel's actual belief. In other words, South Vietnam claimed lives of 81,000 individuals between 1954-1975. These numbers ranged from 57,000 to 284,000. Benjamin Valentino's death rate is between 110,000 to 310,000, and it was considered a "potential example" of counter-guerrilla mass killings by U.S.A. South Vietnamese troops at the time. The CIA's Phoenix Program, which included U.S.A., South Vietnamese security personnel, was designed to remove the Viet Cong's alleged political device. It was responsible for killing between 26,369 - 41,000 people. The unidentified number of innocent citizens were also hurt by it.

South Vietnamese POWs as well as civilian hostages were often subjected to physical and mental abuse.

Augustus F. Hawkins of Congress and William R. Anderson, both American physicians, saw the detainees held in "tiger boxes" or chained up to their cells. The prisoners were also given poor-quality meals during a 1970 visit at the Con Child Jail. The jail was also visited by a group American doctors who found several convicts with conditions related to abuse and pushed immobility.

The International Red Cross documented numerous instances of abuse before the captives were surrendered to South Vietnamese authorities. They had been visiting transit detention center under American guidance in 1968/69.

In partnership with CIA, the South Vietnamese federal government tortured individuals.

South Korean troops were also implicated in war criminal offences. One validated incident was the Phong Nht/Phong Nht slaughter, where the second Marine Brigade allegedly killed between 69-79 villagers on

February 12, 1968 at Phong Nht Town in Ban District in Qung Nam Province. The South Korean forces may have also committed other atrocities, such as the Binh Tai massacre, Ha My massacre, or the Bnh Ha murder.

Ami Perdahzur argues that terrorists should be considered non-state actors and that targeted killings have contributed to civilian deaths.

www.ingramcontent.com/pod-product-compliance
Lightning Source LLC
Chambersburg PA
CBHW050411120526
44590CB00015B/1919